First Person Singular

By Florence Ryerson and Colin Clements

LADIES ALONE
EIGHT COMEDIES

ALL ON A SUMMER'S DAY
SEVEN PLAYS

FIRST PERSON SINGULAR
A BOOK OF MONOLOGUES

First Person Singular

(A BOOK OF MONOLOGUES)

BY

Florence Ryerson

AND

Colin Clements

WITH A FOREWORD BY

May Robson

Samuel French

NEW YORK   TORONTO   LOS ANGELES

1937

MANUFACTURED IN THE UNITED STATES OF AMERICA
BY THE VAIL-BALLOU PRESS, INC., BINGHAMTON, N. Y.

For
RITA VALLELY

Our thanks are due to the Editors of The
Pacific Saturday Night, The Detroit *News,*
The New York *Sun, Life, Woman's World,*
Rob Wagner's *Script,* The *Emerson Quarterly,*
The New York *Saturday Review of Literature,*
The Los Angeles *Times,* and The American
Kennel Gazette, for permission to reprint such
of these sketches and verses as have appeared in
their pages; thanks are also due D. Appleton-
Century Company for permission to paraphrase
a chapter of *Mild Oats.*

FOREWORD

Of late I have often wondered why there were not more published monologues. Certainly nothing is better suited to the spirit of the age than the sharp, crisp—I might call it "streamlined"—character sketch done in the first person singular.

It is good, not only for use in a regular program, but also for reading aloud, or, indeed, for reading to oneself.

A chance remark to this effect, uttered under the spreading trees of Shadow Ranch, led my dear friends, Florence and Colin, to writing sketches, first for their own amusement and ours, then, later, for publication, platform, and radio use.

As godmother to this little collection of monologues, I wish it a fair sailing; and to all of you who do them—good luck and many encores!

MAY ROBSON

Beverly Hills,
California.

CONTENTS

First Person Singular

CRYSTAL CLEAR

SCENE: *The dining room of the Penniforth home.*

(MRS. EVELYN PENNIFORTH *arrives, breathless. She carries a bag and gloves. Her hat is extremely frivolous.*)

John, darling, I'm *so* sorry I'm late! I'll skip the soup, Nellie. Just bring my plate. I couldn't get away . . . the club was so packed. And no potatoes, Nellie. It's potatoes I don't eat this week, isn't it? Parsnips? All right, no parsnips. Oh, there aren't any? Well then, *that's* all right!

John— Just wait until I get off my hat. . . . (*She takes off her hat and puts it down on the table beside her bag and gloves, then sits down.*) There! John, darling, I give you my word that woman is wonderful. Simply wonderful! The things she does to your mind!

What? Oh, the speaker at the club. Madam— Madam— What's her name? Now, isn't that ridiculous? It'll come to me in a minute. Anyway, she's Polish . . . which makes her practically international. I mean, she's got a sort of cosmopolitan point of view, because the Poles never know exactly *what* they are . . . Russian, or German, or—what was that other country? Anyway, they never know. That's what makes them so fascinating!

What? Why, *Current Events,* of course! Don't you remember when I got that twenty-five dollars from you for the course? Well, you certainly ought to remember! The things you said about women's minds! If we hadn't been going out to dinner, I wouldn't have spoken to you all evening.

Oh, Nellie! Hot biscuits? How lovely! It's marvelous! Her mind, I mean. Madam What-cha-ma-call-it's mind. Why, she has all of Europe at her finger tips! And Asia, too. And China. No honey, Nellie? I just wish you could hear what she does to China! Oh, well, jelly will do. Blackberry? Oh, currant.

"Currant." That reminds me! John, she doesn't want it called "Current Events." She wants it called "Current History." Yes, "Current History." Because it *is* history, you know. Even if it's happening to us right now, it's *still* history. And the way she tells about it . . . my dear, it's miraculous! Simply miraculous! Europe . . . Asia . . . Africa . . . it's all crystal clear to me! I give you my word, John, crystal clear!

I wouldn't eat those, if I were you. You know they always disagree with you. Well, of course, if you want to sit up all night just for a few pickled walnuts. . . .

What? Well—first, she talked about America.

Yes. She doesn't scorn America. Not at all. She says it's really quite important. Of course, not as much as we all think, but still . . . fairly important. So she gives it three minutes.

"Minutes." Do remind me to call Lila to-night—about the Junior League. I've lost the minutes of the last meeting.

Where was I? Oh, yes. Madam says the president's fishing. Or was it congress? Anyway, the situation's critical—so maybe they all went. And there are some strikes. Yes, in the Middle West . . . something to do with automobiles . . . and window glass, I think it was. But of course you get all that over the radio. The really interesting part was Europe. All the secret things you don't read, because nobody knows 'em except a few big diplomats and Madam. Well . . . because she knows them all intimately.

John! I think it's disgusting of you to suggest such a thing! And where Nellie could hear you, too. Well, I don't think it's funny. Not a bit. And, anyway, she's at least sixty.

What? Well, *Europe*. Let me see. . . . She said Europe is heading toward a war. Yes, *toward* it. It may come this year, and it may come next, or the year after. It depends upon what the diplomats do. And they aren't quite sure themselves, yet. If they do one thing, it'll be *yes*. If they do another, it won't be. At least, she said something like that.

And then there'll be trouble in the Balkans. You know, all those little countries down at the bottom of the map. Bulgardia, and Slavonia—I think it is—and Transylvania, and Czecho—or isn't Czecho-Slovakia part of the Balkans? I'm never sure. You can look it up after dinner. This is delicious, Nellie. Lots better than the last time. Creamier. Anyway, she said there'd be trouble there.

And England is worrying about India. And Japan is mad at China. And Germany is arming. Oh, she says Germany is arming and arming . . . and so is Italy. She said we should watch them. Keep our eyes right on them. And Manchuria, too. And she said something about Bolivia. Or maybe it was about Liberia. I couldn't hear very well—because Laura Wells was showing me her new hat. Yellow, my dear —with the most poisonous green carbuncle things right here, and a sort of stick-up-'em on top. Wouldn't you think she'd know better?

Anyway, they're having a new king, or forming a republic or something—which may affect the whole European situation adversely, or perhaps it will make it better. We can't tell until it happens. But no matter what it is, we'll have the satisfaction of knowing we saw it coming, and that's such a comfort. Why? Well, really, John, if you can't see it for yourself, I'm sure I can't explain *why*.

Yes, Nellie, coffee in the drawing room. And I'll take cream in mine to-night. I'm just a little tired after the lecture. (*She rises and moves toward the drawing-room door.*) But it was such an intellectual treat. And *now* aren't you ashamed of what you said about women's minds, John? I'll be able to come home every Wednesday and tell you just what to think about everything. . . . (*As she exits.*) It's such a joy to have the whole world-situation clear as crystal!

STREAMLINE

Scene: *The living room of the Penny residence, Christmas morning.*

(James Penny, *talking to his small son, enters. His wife is presumably trailing slightly in the rear.*)

Well! Well! Well! Now let's see what Santa Claus has brought us. Whew! Is that a tree or is that a tree? I'll say it is! And look at all the presents! I guess the old boy must have just about broken his back! Yes. A scooter. A baseball and bat. And some books. Well, look at these!

Put down that bat, Junior—you'll break something—and look at the pretty pictures in these nice books.

What? Well, I wondered when you'd notice *that,* young man! It sort of hit my eye first thing. It's sure a big box . . . a whopping big box! I wonder what it could possibly be?

Well! Well! Well! It's a train! A real, honest-to-goodness, streamlined electric train! Santa Claus certainly knew what somebody wanted! Oh, you did? Well, that just goes to show you it pays to write letters—even up to the North Pole. Of course he lives at the North Pole. He's always lived up there—so's to get the reindeer for his sled.

Well—uh—aviators *have* flown over the pole. No, they haven't seen Santa Claus. I don't know why he doesn't fly in an airplane. Of course it'd be quicker. . . . Now, now, that's enough about that! We want to get this good old train out and put into working, don't we?

What's that, Jane? Yes, yes, we will. . . . You be careful now, Junior, and don't get the floor all littered up. Better gather up that paper and excelsior and carry them over to the waste basket while papa gets out the train. . . .

Well! Well! *Well!* This certainly is a great little model! Look, Jane. Look! The engine—all streamlined—and four passenger cars . . . and two freight . . . and a caboose! That's called a caboose, Junior. Oh, I don't know, just because it's called that, I guess. I don't know why. No—no, don't touch it! It isn't ready yet. You gather up the rest of the papers.

Of course I know it's his, Jane! But I've got to get it fixed for him, haven't I? It isn't like the old trains you used to pull on a string . . . or wind up . . . it's electrical, and you can't expect a child of his age— There's a wad of excelsior you dropped, Junior. Pick it up, and then move the box. Papa wants to lay out the tracks.

Why, hello, Charlie! Glad you dropped in. Say good-morning to Uncle Charlie, Junior. Yes, Santa

Claus was pretty good to us, wasn't he? We're fixing up Junior's train. It's the very newest model. Streamlined, see? The clerk at Milterns' said we could add to it.

What, Junior? Well—uh—I know because . . . well, because Santa Claus told me the man said that. Yes, Santa Claus buys some things at Milterns'. Well . . . I talked to him out the window. Wh—oh, never mind about that now, papa's busy with these tracks.

No! No! No! Not like that! You're doing it all wrong! I'll tell you, suppose you just take them out and hand them to papa, and then he'll get it right. Careful now!

Well, no, Charlie, I don't think we need any help. Well . . . of course . . . if you insist—but don't start at this end. I've sort of got a plan for this end. Start over there.

What, Jane? I can't hear—what? Why, of course it'll have to go across the room. You can't spread out forty feet of track in just a little space! I was figuring on taking it all around there . . . and under the couch . . . then through this tunnel. Isn't this some tunnel, Charlie? And then putting the station over there by the front door. People can step over it when they come in, can't they? Well, if they don't want to, then they can keep out of the room.

No! No, Junior! Don't try to hitch them together. Papa'll tend to that when he finishes laying the tracks.

Tell you what, here's a book of instructions—all full of pictures—you just take it and sit in that chair and read it until papa and Uncle Charlie get the whole thing ready for you.

For heaven's sake, Jane, what are you doing? Well, if I'd wanted the switch there I'd have put it there! Now you've gone and got it all mixed up! Women never know anything about electricity. What? Well . . . all right . . . you can lay out the station if you want to. No, don't touch the round-house. I've got ideas for that.

There now, I guess the track's all together . . . enough so we can try it out, anyway. No, Junior, we're not ready for you yet. You just stay there in that chair and watch.

Charlie, I've already said I don't want the switch there! I want it here! I don't care if it is! Say, whose streamline is this, anyway?

Jane, I don't think that's a very nice thing to say! And right in front of J-u-n-i-o-r! How do you expect him to have any respect— Junior, look out! You almost stepped on it! Listen, if you can't keep quiet you'll have to go to your room!

I'm fully aware it's Christmas morning, Jane. Ouch! I certainly should be, with a Christmas tree scratching my neck!

Junior, don't pucker your face like that. Papa's just trying to fix it for you. See! It's all laid out. Now all we have to do it to take this connection and stick it into the plug . . . like that . . . and then throw this switch. . . .

Look! Lo—ok! Junior! Charlie! It's starting! It's going! Around and around! Look, Jane! Through the tunnel . . . over the bridge . . . and— Oh, boy! Oh, boy! Is that a train!

No, Junior . . . go 'way . . . go 'way—papa's playing with it now!

BALANCING THE BUDGET

SCENE: *The living room of the Virgil Weeks house.*

(MRS. WINIFRED PRINGLE WEEKS *speaks.*)

Yes, Virgil . . . yes . . . of course I hear you, perfectly. But the radio's making so much noise I don't know what you're saying. All right, I'll turn it down. But you don't really get the full effect of that modern music when it's too soft. Why, of course it's modern music. Well . . . because it hasn't any tune. When it isn't like music at all, you know it's *modern* music.

Oh, Virgil . . . not to-night! I don't care if it *is* the fifth of the month, the bills aren't all in yet. Well, the bill for repairing the vacuum cleaner, for instance. I tried to get hold of the man when I went to market to-day, but— Oh, that reminds me! Did I tell you? Clara Hanniford and Sydney are coming over to-morrow night for bridge. I saw her at the market to-day, and she said Mary Jane had bought a new Buick, with green wheels.

Why, Virgil Weeks, I am not! Nothing of the kind! Why should I want to change the subject? I'm exactly as anxious to get that wretched budget balanced as you are. Really more so. Only, I don't keep harping on things the way you do. I'm the kind of a person who can do something without continually talking about it.

But I *am* getting my account book! What else do you think I'm doing? For goodness' sake, don't shout at me like that, or I'll never be able to find it! Of course I have a regular place to keep it. The only trouble is, it's never in its place. Simply never. I honestly think it deliberately hides! Oh, here it is! How it ever got back of the radiator I can't imagine!

Oh, Virgil, stop being so impatient! I have to get a pencil, don't I? Or do you expect me to add everything up in my head?

As a matter of fact, I could—if I set my mind to it. Go on and laugh, if you like. I stood at the top of my class in mathematics. Absolutely the top. Used to work out all those problems about cubes and cones and parameters and things just for the fun of it. Here's a pencil. Oh, de-ar, the point's broken. It *would* be! And I squared the circle quicker than any girl in high school. Or any boy, either.

I didn't say I could do it now. It's something you get out of practice of. Like riding a bicycle. Or roller skating. I certainly never will forget that night at the rink—

All right, I won't! But you *were* a scream. When you knocked Ella Morgan down and sat on her— I didn't say you knocked her down on purpose! Of course not. I was just simply using it to illustrate the fact that you can't go on squaring a circle without keeping up your practice.

Oh, are you ready? Well, why didn't you say so? I've just been waiting for you. Now here's my account book . . . check book . . . bills. . . .

What? Well, no, I haven't exactly entered everything. That is, not quite everything. Some of the items I just jotted down on these little slips and scraps of paper. No, you can't tell anything by that, because some of 'em I've entered and some of 'em I haven't —and I'm not sure which is which.

Let me see . . . seven, eighty-nine. That ought to be easy to find. Yes, there it is! And fourteen, ninety-two. Why on earth is that so familiar? Of course . . . "In 1492, Columbus sailed the ocean blue." I used to be awfully good in history, too. Almost as good as in mathematics. And logic . . . I was simply wonderful in logic.

Can you find any three, fifty-five? It looks like "hair oil." But I never buy hair oil . . . so it must be olive . . . no . . . wait—"car oiled." That's what it is! "Car oiled." It really ought to come out of you, don't you think? Gas comes out of me, and cleaning and tires, but oil comes out of you—like valves and servicing. But accidents come out of both of us. You remember, we agreed on that last month.

Oh, that reminds me! There's a dented fender here somewhere . . . somewhere. There it is! And here's a poker, and two fly swatters. I clipped them together because I didn't know— You might say the poker is house money, but you're sure to use it in the grill, and the grill's garden, which comes out of you. Then the fly swatters are used on the porch as much as in the house, which makes them both outside and inside. What? You'll take them? Well . . . perhaps you'd better, because I haven't enough money, any-way.

Oh, Virgil, I wish you'd stop jumping at conclusions! I didn't say I'd overdrawn. I just said I hadn't quite enough to cover things . . . so just a few of the bills didn't get paid.

Of course I plan to pay them! Why . . . out of this month's allowance. Well, why not? I paid some of this month's out of last month's—that's why I ran short.

I'm sure I don't see why you have to act as though I sent the bills to *myself* just to annoy you! Indeed you do, Virgil. And it isn't as though I'm the least bit extravagant. Why, only this morning I saw a hat . . . blue, with the most adorable bunch of French carrots on the side . . . just right for my new suit . . . and I didn't buy it, because I knew I was running short.

I don't see what good it all does, anyway—eternally adding up and adding up! You don't have a penny more when you get through. No, it isn't. It's worse. Because this way you *know* you're broke. The other way you don't. Well, personally, I think that's a very strange way to look at it—wanting to know when you're broke. It's positively morbid.

I *am* going to add them up! That is, if you'll just stop nagging. . . . Eight and ten is eighteen . . . seven . . . carry nine . . . seventy-two, plus five . . . six and twenty-three. . . . There it is! Or—or is it?

I couldn't possibly have spent seventeen hundred and sixty-eight dollars, could I? I'm sure I couldn't, because I only had a hundred and fifty—you know I did—but there it is, right in black and white!

What? Oh—of course—it's in the wrong column, isn't it? And I added in the date. That makes a difference. And the decimal point. . . .

Virgil! Virgil! Do you see what that means? It means I haven't gone over a single, solitary penny! It means I still have five dollars and seventeen cents in the bank!

Virgil! I'm going down to-morrow—I'm going down very first thing—and get that hat!

FIRST WIFE TO SECOND WIFE

SCENE: *A quiet corner at a noisy cocktail party.*

(MRS. ALTHEA BAINBURY *is talking to* MRS. HENRY BAINBURY. *She wears a long string of beads and is smoking a cigarette. Her hands are never at rest, they betray her inner nervousness.*)

My dear, I'm so glad to talk to you—so *glad!* You don't believe that, do you? You can't, because you aren't used to people like me. But I do, truly I do—mean it, I mean. I mean every word of it.

I was so glad when I heard Bert had asked you and Harry to come to-day. Of course, he didn't know Helen had already asked me . . . and when they found out—well, you can imagine! Helen nearly died. That's what she told me over the phone . . . practically died and was buried!

But I told her I didn't mind a bit. Said I'd love to meet Harry's little bride. And I meant it. I've wanted to meet you for a long time, and tell you I wasn't in the least bitter. Why, I'm actually grateful to you. I feel I ought to *thank* you . . . because you've done me the greatest favor any woman ever did another. Why, if it wasn't for you, I'd probably still be married to Harry. . . .

No, Pedro, no more cocktails. Splendid houseboy they've got. Had him for years. I remember when Harry and I used to come here to dinner. . . . Oh, Pedro, wait! I think I'll change my mind. Just *one* more. I do like Filipinos, don't you? They're so piquant. Have you one with vermuth? No, that's too fattening! A Bronx . . . no . . . an Old-fashioned. Thank you. I'm not at all—but I think they're safest. Well—here's your health, Ann!

You don't mind if I call you "Ann," do you, dear? I feel as though I know you so well. That's a terribly conventional remark, isn't it? And we're terribly *un*-conventional. Talking this way, I mean. Most women would be tearing each other's hair out. But I'm not that way. I do the most unconventional things. Absolutely the most—but I suppose Harry's told you. . . .

Oh, he doesn't? Well, perhaps it's better . . . although the psychologists *do* say if you avoid talking about a thing it shows you're afraid of it. But, of course, Harry couldn't be afraid of reawakening anything. Not when he has a lovely little bride like you.

No, I'm not flattering you, my dear. I say just the same thing behind your back. I was talking to Rose the other day— But of course you know who she is! Rose—at Madame Hélène's—the girl who touches up your hair.

I said to Rose, "If you could just get half as good

a permanent on me as you've put on dear Ann—"
Only, I called you Mrs. Bainbury, of course. You
can't imagine how funny it seems to call anybody else
Mrs. Bainbury. Really *immoral.* I said, "If you could
only put as good a permanent on me, I'd swoon with
delight." But she said she couldn't, because thick
curly hair never takes as good a wave as the thin,
straight kind. And the same goes for henna. Oh, you
don't? But I was sure she said—

Oh, Helen darling, how *are* you? Yes, we're having a beautiful time. Truly we are. We have so much
in common. Oh, no—I couldn't! I've had several
. . . two, at least. I couldn't . . . really I couldn't!
Well . . . if you insist—just one little Manhattan,
and I'll sip it. (*She takes a glass and drinks.*) Leave
one for Ann, too. Oh, yes, I call her Ann. It's a beautiful name, and a beautiful little girl. . . .

Of course you want one, Ann, of course. Well—
then, just leave it there on the table and perhaps she'll
change her mind. And thank you, Helen, for bringing
us togezzer—I mean, together.

(*She turns back to* ANN.)

Whew, it's hot in here! Makes you terribly thirsty,
doesn't it? It doesn't? It does me. Well, if you're not
going to . . . you don't mind? Thanks.

(*She takes the second cocktail which* HELEN *left
on the table.*)

Oh, hello, Peg! Yes, it is, isn't it? No, it isn't, is it?
Yes, indeed! No, indeed! You haven't met Mrs.

Bainbury. She's Barry's bittle lide . . . I mean, Larry's rittle hide . . . I mean, Harry's— Oh, you *know* her? Why, of course, we're having a *beautiful* visit.

My dear—did you see the way she looked at me? I suppose she can't un'erstan' my talking to you like this . . . and not hating you at all. Because I don't. Truly I don't. I'm so much happier as I am. A thousand times happier.

Thank you, Pedro—jus' one little one more, because it's so warm. . . .

Wha' was I sayin'? Oh, yes, I was sayin'—I was sayin' I never was so happy . . . I could sing . . . jus' to be free. To know I c'n go anywhere I wan' to . . . not to have to listen to Harry tell 'bout office. It's you has t' do that. 'S you, Ann—dear—darling Ann—little Orphan Annie! The laugh's on you, Orphan Annie! (*She begins to laugh hysterically.*) The laugh's on you! Because I'm the lucky one, see? I'm the lucky one—and you—you're fooled. . . . (*Her voice begins to change, to become venomous.*) You nasty thieving little cat! No, you can't get away . . . I won't let you. You're goin' to stay here while I tell you jus' what I think!

Oh, hello, Harry! Jus' been talkin' to your wife— to Ann—dear, darlin' l'le Annie. Wha'? I don' care if they do hear me . . . I wan' 'em to hear me! (*She calls wildly.*) Come on! Come on, everybody, an' hear . . . because I'm—I'm gonna tell 'bout a little thievin' sneak who stole my husban'! Lef' me all alone—alone—alone. I wanna die! I wanna kill her! Kill her 'n' die. . . .

(*She suddenly looks around, then speaks with quiet pathos.*)

Oh, my God—what'm I saying? What am I saying? Take me home . . . Harry . . . darling . . . take me home. . . .

PEACE ON EARTH *

SCENE: *The Follansbee living room during a meeting of the Springdale Community Christmas Pageant committee.*

(MRS. ORMA WILMETTE FOLLANSBEE *sits at a small table. She is wearing a pair of pince-nez on a chain and holds a wooden gavel in her hand. She knocks two or three times on the table, then looks around brightly.*)

I believe everyone is here except Mr. Jones and Mrs. Davis, so we might as well call the committee to order. Yes. Now if all you gentlemen who are smoking will just move over by the open window. . . . I hope you ladies won't find it too cold, but the smoke has to go *some*where. (*Raising her voice, and speaking to the right.*) Mr. Peevy . . . Mr. Peevy, I said if all the gentlemen who are smo— That's right. (*In a lower tone, to the left.*) Yes. Deafer every day. But pageants always seem to bring that sort of people out . . . you've noticed it?

---

* Suggested by an incident in *Mild Oats,* published by D. Appleton-Century Company; copyright, 1933, by Florence Ryerson Clements and Colin Clements.

21

I beg your pardon? Oh, yes. If any of the ladies really care to smoke, they may. Of course I never do myself. I've always felt it was just a little— But I flatter myself I'm broad-minded.

Yes, Mr. St. John, quite, quite ready. (*She takes up a sheet of paper.*) Now what have you brought us? Oh, the order of the episodes. Um-m-m, let me see. (*She puts on her glasses and reads.*)

"The Nativity." "The Coming of the Shepherds and the Three Kings." We're one king short. Make a note of that, will you please, Mr. Conkling? "Mediaeval Yuletide." "Christmas in France. England. Spain. And China." We had to put that last in because of all those costumes the Community Arts had left over from the *Yellow Jacket*. "The Waits and Minstrels." That's the Methodist choir—they won't sing with the Episcopalians. Don't ask me why. Something to do with vestments . . . or maybe it was incense. "Christmas in Italy. Holland." That's my niece's dancing class. They're doing a wooden-shoe dance. "Christmas in New England." "Grand Finale," with the two bands, and the Swing Music Association.

Very nice, Mr. St. John. Very nice indeed. (*Loudly, to right.*) I beg your pardon, Mr. Peevy? But I *did* read it. Here, perhaps you'd like to. (*More softly, to left.*) *That*'ll keep him busy.

Now . . . if you're all agreed on the order of

episodes, we'll take up our other problems. (*She studies her list.*) Let me see . . . the first thing is "goats." Yes . . . that's right. "Goats." Mr. St. John says that he can't get the *feel* of the Nativity scene without sheep, and there isn't a sheep in town, except at the butcher's—and of course they're skinned. But he says goats will do. He's used them before.

What? Oh, no! He hobbles them! Isn't that right, Mr. St. John? I thought so. They don't butt when they're hobbled.

Now, have any of you any goats? No, I thought not. Well, do any of you know anyone who has any goats . . . or do you know anyone who knows anyone who— (*She looks around expectantly.*) Well, in that case, I'd better appoint a sub-committee. Mr. Conkling and Miss Tripp. I beg your pardon? Oh, of course, you're snow fairies, aren't you? And reindeer. We can't ask any more of you. Well, then, Mr. Peevy, there's something you can do. (*She raises her voice.*) Mr. Peevy, I'm putting you on the goat committee. Not ghost! Goat. To get our goats . . . please. Mr. Conkling, you explain to him. (*To left.*) So trying!

Good evening, Mrs. Davis. We thought you had forgotten the meeting. Oh, the Wednesday Club. Why? What was the trouble? They were? Well, I'm sure I don't know why they should feel insulted! No, indeed. We're splitting the Nativity between the Elks and the Rotarians, and the Lady Foresters are doubling up with the Y.M.C.A. in Santa Claus Land. I don't see why the Wednesday Club can't divide France with the Colonial Dames.

Well, if they don't know each other, let them get acquainted. That's what pageants are for . . . to get people acquainted. Why, half the women who aren't speaking now didn't even know each other last month.

What's that, Mr. Peevy? You don't know any goats? But that's why I put you on the committee. To go out and find them. There must be goats somewhere. Just ask around! Ask around!

Now, Mrs. Davis, you'll have to be firm with the Wednesday Club ladies. Tell them they'll have to split France or—oh, yes—and tell them the skirts must be not more than ten inches from the ground. Ten inches—that's final.

Let me see, what's next? (*She studies her list.*) Um-m-m. "Table salt." Now that doesn't seem to convey anything to me. (*She peers at her list intently.*) It's scribbled so. It wouldn't be "tabouret" would it? Or "troubadour"? No . . . we have all our troubadours. Did I tell you the Glee Club had taken that over? And very nicely, too! "Tableau." That's it! "Tableau." The idea of my forgetting! It's very important. The Chamber of Commerce had a joint meeting with the Merchants' Association, and they've offered to put up the grand stand if we'll run in a tableau representing Home Products.

Yes, Mr. St. John, I explained that, but they seemed to think it would fit all right. I'm sure we can tie it in with the Christmas idea—not in the Nativity scene —but perhaps in Santa Claus Land.

Oh, Mr. Cushing, make a note: "Jones—aurora borealis." Never mind anything more. I'll know what it means. "Jones—aurora borealis."

Let's get back to the subject in hand. Don't you think Santa Claus could sort of be distributing Springdale Home Products from his sleigh? Of course, it's a little hard to work in Miss Prosperity. Oh, did I forget to mention it? They want Lulla Bryson—yes, she's Mr. Bryson's daughter. (*In a louder voice.*) Bryson, Mr. Peevy! Bryson. President of the First National. (*In a normal tone again.*) They want her to represent Prosperity—in gold tights and spangles. (*Louder.*) No, Mr. Peevy . . . not *Mr.* Bryson. His daughter.

Which reminds me, Mrs. Knapp—you're New England, aren't you? Yes, of course. Well . . . you'll simply have to tell the Pilgrim Mothers that they can't wear satin. Absolutely not. Nor taffeta, either. And no silk stockings.

What's that, Mr. St. John? You're right. Absolutely right! Mrs. Knapp, did you hear that? No painted finger nails. That goes for everyone—especially in the Nativity. Please make a note of that, Mr.

Cushing. (*She speaks louder.*) I said no painted finger nails in the Nativity, Mr. Peevy. Not tails . . . *nails!*

Oh, Mr. Jones, I'm so glad you've come at last! Did you get the aurora borealis? Good! And the Indians? And the gondolas? Splendid! How about the elephant and camel? (*To the others.*) For the Wisemen, you know. (*To* Mr. Jones.) Just an elephant and donkey? I see. . . . Republican and Democrat. Well, I suppose we could paint over the flags, but I did so want a camel. (*Louder.*) Oh, no, Mr. Peevy, I didn't mean that! I *never* smoke. (*Lower.*) Isn't it weird the way he understands sometimes, and at others—you have to be so careful. . . .

Yes, Jane? Miss Brady? I'll take it here. (*Into the telephone.*) Hello. Hello, Miss Brady. What? They have? Oh, *dear.* (*To the others.*) The Peace Society is having a horrible row with the Christian Endeavor, and they simply won't do England together. (*Into phone.*) What? Yes, I'm telling them now. (*To the others.*) Neither side will give in. Mr. St. John, you'll simply have to write another episode.

I have it! Little Susy Watson's mother's been pestering me about her doing a Spanish dance. She does the split, you know . . . and three cartwheels. Yes, I know we have Christmas in Spain already. Yes, that's a splendid idea! (*Into telephone.*) Everything's settled! Yes . . . Mr. St. John is going to write another episode. Christmas in Mexico. That's right. How's the rehearsal going? It is? That's too bad—but just keep on keeping on. That's the spirit! Keep on keeping on. . . .

(*She hangs up the receiver and looks around, a trifle wildly.*)

Now where were we? Oh, yes—my list—let me see—I have one more item. It looks . . . it looks like "Peace on Earth." Now what could I have meant by that? What do you suppose— (*In a loud voice.*) I said "Peace on Earth," Mr. Peevy. "Peace on Earth."

MIKE

SCENE: *The living room of the Bennett house.*

(JACKIE BENNETT *enters with a deprecating air. He wears a cap. His hands are deep in his pockets. He speaks.*)

Oh, there you are, Dad. Gee, I'm glad! I wanted to— Sure, Mom . . . I'm takin' it off. (*He takes off his cap and flings it out of scene, without looking.*) Oh . . . gee, Mom, I'm sorry! Well, how could I know the ol' vase was there? And, anyways, it's just the one Aunt Tillie gave you. Dad always said he wished some'n' 'ud break it. But you *did,* Dad. I've heard you say it—lots of times. Why, I didn't mean to contradict. I just said—

Huh? I mean, yes, sir? Oh, you mean that kind of —of a scratchin' sound? And whinin'? That? Well, that—uh—uh—that's what I came in to tell you 'bout.

Oh, no, sir! It isn't a dog. That is . . . not exactly a dog. I mean, not a *big* dog. He's just a—a puppy dog. (*He calls over his shoulder.*) Shush! Hush, Mike! That's his name—Mike. Shush!

Huh? I mean, yes, sir? Well—no—he doesn't be-

long to any of the boys. That is—well—uh—he sort
of belongs to me. . . .

Yes, sir. No, sir. Mmm-huh. I mean, yes, sir. I
know you did. But that was last year—after old
Blackie died. I thought—maybe—well, there's the
empty dog house, and it seemed kind of a shame to
waste it.

Shush, Mike! I'm comin'!

He won't always make a noise like that, Mom. It's
just because he wants to get in to me. He's crazy
about me, Dad. Wait! I'll show you. . . . (*He
opens a door.*) Here, Mike! Here! Down, boy!
Down! No, don't jump up. Down! He won't hurt
you, Dad. It's just because he likes you. He likes you,
too, Mom.

Aw, gee, I'm sorry—but he couldn't know he had
mud on his paws. Mike, drop that pillow! Drop it!
Lie down! I haven't got him very well trained yet.
But I will. He's goin' to learn to sit up, and lie down,
and jump through a hoop. Lie down! Down! There,
that's right. Now you stay there.

Huh? I mean, yes, ma'am? Well, he's—he's—the
man I got him from didn't exactly say what kind he
was, but I think he's a sort of a hunting dog . . .
crossed with air-a-dale.

No, *sir!* He isn't a cur. Why, his mother's half
thoroughbred! Yes, she is, too. On her mother's side.
The man said so.

Ma'am? (*Reluctantly.*) Well . . . I don't exactly know the man's name. He doesn't live around here. He lives down across the tracks. He's—he's a kind of a colored man.

Aw, gee, Dad, it's mean to say that! Right where Mike can hear you. Of course he understands! He understands every word anybody says to him. And colored men have just as good dogs as anybody—an' he's a beautiful dog. Look at his eyes. An' the way his tail curls up. An' his paws won't look so big as they do now when he kind of grows up to 'em.

Oh, no, sir, he isn't goin' to get great big. That is, not so very big. Not a lot bigger'n old Blackie was. That's why I thought he'd be just right . . . he'll fit the dog house.

No, no, Mom, he didn't make that spot! Why, he couldn't of! I've had him right— Somebody's just spilled some water . . . when they was fillin' the vases or somethin'. All right, I'll take him out. I'll take him out—an' tie him up in Blackie's old house.

Aw, Dad, don't say that! You can't—why, I—I got to have a dog. Honest I have! All the other boys —I'm not answerin' back! I'm just tryin' to tell you how— Down, Mike! Down! Aw, gee, Dad—I can't take him back! I can't! I wasn't tellin' you the truth. That is, it wasn't exactly a lie . . . 'cause there *was* a colored man . . . but he didn't give me Mike. He— he was givin' him to a man to take to the pound. You know what they do down there . . . they kill them! They were goin' to kill my dog—Mike. They'd kill him now, if you make me take him back. An' he's a good dog. A swell dog! Look at the way he's lickin' your hand. Look at his eyes. They look the way Mom's did when she had that fever. You remember, the time we sat up all night 'n' held her hands . . . an' we thought she was goin' to die?

Please, Dad, please! Don't make me take back my dog. I don't want him killed. Please! Please! Please. . . .

You will? I can? Oh, Dad . . . Mom . . . thanks. Aw, gee! Aw, *gee!*

Yeah, I'll mop it up . . . an' I'll take the dime 'n' get hamburger . . . an' I'll clean out the dog house, an' build a fence! Yeah, an' get A in arithmetic! Mike! Mike! Come on, Mike! Good old dog! Come on. . . .

TALES OUT OF SCHOOL

THE LITTLE GIRL NEXT DOOR SHARES HER SECRETS

SCENE: *Over the back fence.*

(*The* LITTLE GIRL *next door speaks.*)

CLEAN STREETS

Our gutters are the very worst
    Of any street in town;
If I had only seen them first
    Before we settled down
Into this house we're going to stay in,
I would have brought some mud to play in.

SPLASH!

I've often sat all by myself
And wondered what was on the shelf
In papa's study closet. Well . . .
I found out! Promise you won't tell,
But if you go and look, I think
You'll see that what it *was* was ink.

32

DAY DREAM

I wish I was a little stone
Out somewhere in the woods alone;
With no one there to bother me,
I'd only have to sit and *be*.

LIONS

There's lions in our pepper tree,
When I'm up there they play with me!

Don't you believe it? Ask our cook.
She'll tell you how the lions look.

Or ask the man who brings the mail,
He's often seen one wag its tail!

But don't ask them when nurse is by,
She'll say it's just another lie.

SUBTRACTION

My mother wants to take a diet:
That makes her cross. If she should try it,
My father says that, fat or slim,
She'll lose two hundred pounds of him.

TEACHER

Our teacher's got a horrid face,
The lines upon her forehead trace
All crosswise in a sort of frown,
And 'round her mouth they're up 'n' down;
But when our principal, Old Schmidt,
Comes in, she pins a smile on it
And says: "Now, children, let's be gay!"
I like her best the other way.

SWEET MAN

I know the very sweetest man,
Who carries off our garbage can;
He's just as friendly as can be,
And loves to stop and talk with me;
My mother doesn't like his smell,
But then she doesn't know him well.

BARBER SHOP

SCENE: *The barber shop of* NICK PANTELLO.

(RUBY, *the manicurist, wears a beaded band across the front of her hair, very large imitation pearls, and is chewing gum. She sits down in a chair and arranges her tray on a table.*)

Well, well, if it ain't Mr. Henry J. Staats in person! I'll start with the right hand. That's it. I thought you'd be out to that place you got on the lake a hot day like this.

Gee, it sure *is* hot. Damp hot. (*She laughs at something* MR. STAATS *has said.*) You would say that! Always a laugh!

Ain't Mr. Staats the great little kidder, Gus? You oughtta heard the one he just pulled. He says it ain't the humidity gets him down, it's the heat!

Huh? The captain and the China-girl? No, I don't think I've heard that one. Mebbe you'd better not tell me. I might split m' lip laughin'. Well, all right . . . I'll take a chance.

A captain of a freight boat? Yeah. Into Peking— Sure I know where Peking is. In Shanghai. No, I haven't heard it . . . honest, I haven't. What'd he say to her? He did? (*She laughs raucously.*) That's a good one!

Oh, Mr. Pantello, y' oughtta get Mr. Staats, here, to tell you his new one about the captain and the China-girl. Yeah, it's a scream! Oh! D' I stick you? Gee, I'm sorry—but you shouldn't ought to make me laugh like that.

Huh? Say, that's darn sweet of you, Mr. Staats, but I can't. Well . . . because I don't eat lunch. No, honest, I don't. I gotta keep my girlish figure—what's left of it. Lost weight? Oh, no. Leastwise, if I have, it's just the heat. Now the other hand. You can soak this one.

Yeah . . . I live in a little apartment up near the brewery. Sure it's hot, but what the— I mean, it's all right. I'm not kickin'.

Say, I can't work on you when you do that! It's *me* that's supposed to be holdin' your hand, see?

Why, Mr. Staats! Did you hear what he said, Gus? He's a clown . . . absolutely a clown! An' I bet you got a wife, too . . . an' mebbe a kid. Oh, is that so? He's got three of 'em, Gus. Two in high school? An' not a gray hair in your head! It's wonderful. Wonderful.

Now you can soak this one. How do you like the new buffer? Well, lot's of my customers are crazy about it.

What's that, Gus? Sure . . . I'll come. You don't

mind if I go into the next room to the phone a minute, do you, Mr. Staats? It—it's kind of important.

(*She rises, takes a few steps to the right. Her
whole expression changes. She loses her smile, grows
suddenly drawn and haggard.*)

Oh, my God, Gus, I hope it ain't bad news about
Ed. Yeah, he was worse this mornin'. Not hemor-
rhagin' . . . but weak. It's this heat. It'll kill him if
it keeps up.

Hello—hello. Yes, this is Mrs. Brady. All right,
I'll wait. . . .

Be a pal, Gus, an' try to keep old Pantello from
seein'. You know how sore he gets if we use the
phone.

Hello—hello. Oh, Doctor, did they have to send
for you? Then he's worse? Yeah . . . I know there
isn't any air. I've tried to find some other place, but
it costs so much to move. (*Over her shoulder.*) Yes,
Mr. Pantello, I'll make it short. (*Into phone.*) Yeah
. . . I'll get it on the way home . . . and the wine
. . . an' I'll rub him . . . an' try to find some other
place. Yeah.

(*She hangs up, and stands looking straight ahead
with a stricken expression, then turns her head as
though someone had come in. She speaks wearily.*)

He's worse, Gus. He's gonna die if I don't do
somethin'! An' there ain't nothin' I can do. Nothin'.
That Staats beast out there. . . . I gotta laugh at

his jokes. Let him hold my hand. Just for the extra tip! An' him with all that dough. . . . I'd like to kill him! Kill him! (*She sobers suddenly.*)

Yes, Mr. Pantello, I'm comin'.

I'm all right, Gus. I can take it. I guess I got to!

(*She manages to force a smile, then hurries back to her table.*)

Well, Mr. Staats, I bet you thought I'd run out on you! I'll do your left hand next. Have you thought up any more laughs?

Oh, Gus told you? Say, he oughtn't to have done that. Because Mr. Pantello don't like it. He thinks the customers won't come if they think they have to be sympathetic . . . an' I can't afford to lose my job. Not right now. Oh, gee, did I jab you? I couldn't see, because—well, thinkin' about Ed up there alone, all day, except for one hour when the district nurse comes, an' the heat, an' no air. . . .

Sa—ay, I didn't mean to unload on you, Mr. Staats. Honest, I didn't. Just forget it, will y'? An' tell me a funny story that will make me laugh, before Pantello sees—

What's that? Aw, Mr. Staats, don't kid me. You can't mean it. You couldn't! But ain't you using it? You're sure your wife wouldn't mind?

Gus, Mr. Staats has . . . well . . . he . . . well, you know the place he's got up on the lake? They ain't going to use it 'cause they're goin' to Europe. He says we can live in the guest cottage—Ed 'n' me.

I can come back and forth to work on the bus. There's a vegetable garden . . . an' a cow that gives butter 'n' eggs . . . an' a man to take care of her.

Aw, say, Mr. Staats, I can't. It's too much. 'Specially with a nurse. I couldn't ever repay you.

(*There is a pause while she listens. Her eyes fill with tears.*)

Well, if you started as poor as that, I guess you know what it means, an' losin' your sister, an' all.

Will I take it? Say, I'm pinchin' myself black 'n' blue to make sure I ain't dreamin'! (*She rises.*) I got to go home 'n' tell Ed. I can't wait! You'll go with me 'n' tell him? Good! Gee . . . I'm sorry, Mr. Staats. Oh, never mind what for. Just sorry for somethin' I said. (*Moving toward the door.*) You're a prince! That's what, a prince! (*As they exit.*)

For cryin' out loud, I never finished your left hand!

I CAN'T MAKE UP MY MIND

I wish my mind were like a bed
And, once made up, would stay smooth spread;

But no, the very least advice
Will muss it up, not once or twice,

But half a dozen times, and then,
I have to make it up again.

SCENE: *The terrace of a country club, while a gradua-tion-class dance is in progress.*

(LINNIE MAE STERRETT *comes out the door with a little rush, giggling, and talking back over her shoulder to her partner.* LINNIE MAE *is seventeen.*)

Oh, oh, oh, you slay me! Absolutely slay me! Dear —oh—dear! I'll die laughing! Positively! (*She quiets down.*) Isn't it heavenly out here? Simply heavenly! That moon? And those stars? I've never seen anything so heavenly in all my life. Absolutely never! Not since I was born, have I ever seen any-thing one half so heavenly . . . or one *quarter!*

I tell you what, let's not go back inside. Let's stay out here. I couldn't dance another step . . . posi-tively not another *step* to-night. At least, not for a minute or two. We can sit here, and sort of rest . . .

40

and get acquainted. I really don't know anything about you, except that you came with Meg Cassidy, and you go to college, and your name is Bill. So if you really want to sit down and get acquainted— Oh, that's adorable of you to say that! Simply adorable!

(*She sits down and stretches out her feet.*)

Oh, boy—ee, does that feel good! I've been on my feet since dawn. Positively! Ever since nine or ten this morning. I was chairman of the decorations committee, you know, and that's a terrible responsibility. I mean, it really is! All the tissue paper and everything. . . . Then, I pledged sandwiches. Some of the girls pledged cake, and some pledged punch, but I pledged sandwiches—and they took hours and hours to do. Positively! They took Helga so long she was late getting dinner.

And the way father *acted!* But I told him you only have a graduation prom once in your life. That is, of course, unless you go to college. You do, don't you? Yes—I know—Meg told me. I'm not sure if I'm going or not.

Well . . . that's simply adorable of you, but I can't seem to make up my mind. It's a terribly big question, don't you think? Someways it means a girl's whole life. Shall she go to college, or shan't she go to college—and if so, which?

The way some girls decide, just because some boy goes to this one or that one, absolutely makes me shudder. I mean, it really does! Just positively shudder clear down my spine, because they may be ruining their whole lives by going to the wrong one, and they don't seem to think anything about it any more than as if they were picking out a new dress.

But some girls are like that. Maybe you've noticed. All sort of frivolous. Never giving a thought to anything except clothes, or parties, or the kind of a permanent they're going to get. Or maybe you like them that way?

I'm glad you don't . . . because, well, because I'm really pretty serious about life. I mean, I really am. But not *awfully* serious. That is, not *too* awfully serious, because, of course, I like to laugh, and dance. . . .

Sometimes I laugh and laugh—I just can't *stop* laughing! And sometimes I dance and dance. . . . Oh, do you think I do? Well, that's absolutely adorable of you to say that, because of course I know all about dancing. I do toe and tap as well as ballroom. Sometimes I think I'll do that instead of go to college. I mean go into it professionally. Go to New York . . . in a night club or a revue or something.

Of course I know it's frightfully difficult to get started, but my dressmaker— Yes. Do you really like it? Well, that's just adorable of you to say that. Anyhow, she has a sister who knows a girl who's in a New York revue—I don't just remember her name, but I know she wears a big hat—and *she* can't even sing. No, nor dance, either. She's just got a back. And legs, of course.

Now, I've got legs and a back and— Oh, aren't you silly! You can't really see it, because mother's absolutely Victorian. I mean *Victorian* . . . and she won't let me wear anything the way I want it. But we might go bathing some time! Anyway, I don't want to boast or anything like that, but I can sing, and dance, too, so I don't see why not. Or even the movies.

Oh, do *you* want to write? Stories, you mean? Well, I think that's the most amazing coincidence! I mean really amazing . . . absolutely unbelievably weird! Because that's exactly what I want to do, too! That is, if I don't dance—or act—or go into the movies.

Of course, father says college would help in writing. He says just studying what other people have written would help. But I don't know. . . . I took Freshman English, and Junior and Senior Composition. You might say I just about covered everything there was to know about literature in high school, and I can't see that it helped a bit . . . all those old Shakespeare plays, and Milton, and—and Hiawatha. What good does it do? That's what I want to know. What do you get out of it except looking up a lot of footnotes about what's a "hautboy," and where is "Arcady"?

Now what I think about writing is— What? Honestly? That's simply too marvelous. It's a even more marvelous coincidence than the other. Positively! Why, it gives me the creeps! Because that's exactly what I think. *Exactly!* You have to live to write. Live. And live. And LIVE. And if you suffer . . . that helps, too.

Of course, a girl can't really *live* like a man. I mean, tramp schooners, and the South Pole, and things like that. But she can keep an apartment in New York. Yes, and go to night clubs, and see life. Because if she doesn't, what's she going to write about? That's what I ask father just about every single solitary day of my life. What is there to write about in a town like this, with only a single street-car line and hardly even one murder a year?

But he won't even hear of the apartment. He's the stubbornest thing. You just wouldn't believe how stubborn he is. Oh, is he? We certainly are alike in lots of ways—our fathers and everything. Doesn't it sort of—well, make you *think?* I mean, the way we like everything the same way . . . and dislike everything the same way? It makes you feel as though— well, as though maybe it *meant* something.

Oh, I think it's adorable of you to say that! Simply adorable! Because— I guess I better not say it. No, no, I wont. I absolutely won't! So don't try to tease me!

Oh—well—all right—if you insist. I hope we're

going to see a lot of each other, too. There now, I've said it!

Let's go on talking about our careers. There's just about absolutely nothing so interesting. Don't you feel that way?

Mother wants me to learn to cook, and sew, and take charge of a house. Things like that. She wants me to get married. Of course, she doesn't exactly come right out and say so, but I can tell what she means. Oh, no, I'm not against marriage—in any sense of the word. In fact, I—well, I'm very broad-minded about marriage versus career. Positively! I wouldn't want to go on without *any* home life. Only, what I say is, learning to cook, and to sew, and to order things from the grocery store—that's something you can learn after you're married as well as before, because then you might as well do that as anything, because there won't be anything else to do. I mean, unless you have a career and get married too. What do you think?

Oh, you do? Well, I guess perhaps you're right. Yes . . . I believe you're absolutely right. Especially if the man has plenty of money so his wife can have a car of her own, and a fur coat—and a diamond bracelet. She wouldn't want to have to do anything then, would she?

Oh! Is that your car out there? Not the roadster with the turn-down top and wire wheels? It *is?* Oh, isn't it simply gorgeous! (*She rises quickly.*) Would

I like to ride in it? Why, I—I'd love it! Simply love it! (*Over her shoulder.*) No, Jimmy, you've got mixed up. This isn't your dance at all. I have the next one with—with— (*To her partner.*) What *is* your name? Oh, yes! Of course! Bill. (*Over her shoulder.*) With Bill, here. Yes, I know I had the last, but I have the next one, too—and the next after that. . . . (*To her partner.*) Oh, come on, let's go before anyone else bothers us.

(*As they leave.*)

What did you say your college is? Oh. Do they take girls? Well, I don't know, but maybe—of course I'm not sure yet—but maybe I *might* decide to go there.

WOMEN CAN'T CARPENTER

Scene: *The kitchen of the J. Walter Ballingford house.*

(Mr. Ballingford *enters, and addresses his wife.*)

Mary! *Mary!* What're you doing up on that ladder? Oh, you are! Well, I'd never have suspected it! In carpentering, the object of using the hammer is to hit the nail upon the head and drive it into the wood. I know I promised to put it up, but I've been exceedingly busy all week. And one doesn't just put up shelves in that casual, off-hand manner. You've got to measure and cut them, and then there are the brackets. I forgot to get them. . . .

Oh, you did? And the nails? H'm! So-o-o, having a hammer and some nails, you thought that was all it took to put up a shelf! If that isn't just like a woman!

My dear, women may vote, they may even be doctors, or lawyers—but have you ever heard of a woman carpenter? No . . . don't try to wriggle out of it, just answer me honestly: Have you *ever* heard of a woman carpenter?

You bet you haven't! Well, then, there must be

some reason, mustn't there? Nothing of the sort! If women were fit to be carpenters, they'd be carpenters.

It hasn't anything to do with ridgepoles! If women were capable of being carpenters, they'd be capable of climbing ridgepoles. It goes much deeper than that. It's because they lack something. No . . . I don't know what it is. Just that *something* which makes carpenters.

My dear girl, I am *not* standing around talking, and I have every intention of putting up the shelf. I can't say just when. No, I'm playing golf this afternoon. Well, of course, if you're going to be unpleasant about it . . .

Give me those hammer and that nails! I mean— Thank you. And now will you please steady the ladder? I know you didn't, but I'm heavier than you are . . . much heavier. Very well, if you want me to break my neck! All right . . . steady it near the top.

There. Now hand me the wood. No . . . wait . . . I think I'd better take off my coat. It binds when I reach. (*He takes off his coat.*) There. That's much better. Now if you'll steady it again, and hand me the wood . . . Easy. Easy, while I try it. Good.

Mary, look, would you mind just climbing up behind me and holding this for a minute? I seem to have got a bit of sawdust in my eye. Yes . . . that's right . . . I think I can get it . . . no . . . I can't. Could you take a look? Well, you can hold the shelf

with one hand. It isn't heavy. All right . . . here
. . . I'll hold it. (*He rolls his eyes up, then down.*)
See anything? Have you—have you got it? Good!
(*He blinks.*) There, that's lots better. Thank you.
All right—here's a kiss. Women never *can* stick to
one thing!

Here, give me that shelf again. Now you can get
down and steady the ladder. No . . . wait . . . the
hammer, and the nails. I was sure I put them in my
pocket. Oh, of course, I took off my coat. Over there.
On the chair.

Thank you, my dear. Now if you'll just watch
closely, I'll give you a little lesson in— This shelf is
too short! Yes . . . at least four inches! You can
see for yourself. I knew they'd get it wrong! What?
Oh, yes, of course it goes the other way. I'd have
noticed it myself in a minute. I was just a trifle con-
fused by— Now what did I do with that hammer? I
think it's in my hip pocket. Is it? Well, I can't reach
around while I'm holding up the shelf! Would you
mind— No, that won't work, because I haven't a
hand to hold the hammer.

I don't think this is any time for jokes, Mary! Besides, there isn't a monkey in the world that could
hold a hammer in his tail and hit a nail. That was a
circus monkey, he was different. And, anyway, it was
probably a fake—just a man dressed up in a monkey
suit.

No . . . that won't work, either! I think perhaps
if I put the brackets in first— No . . . I can't do
that. Because of the cleats, that's why.

Oh, De—lia! Delia! Will you come here a minute?
Mrs. Ballingford is holding the ladder and I need
someone to hold up the shelf while I— Yes, you can,
if you stand on your tiptoes and reach up. That's it.
Up. Up. . . .

Damn it, there go the nails! No, don't bother. I
have two in my— My God, I've swallowed one!
Ugh! Ugh! I must have! It's gone! Ugh! Ugh! No
. . . here it is! It fell on top of the ladder . . . so
that's all right!

What? No! Of course I won't leave it for a regular carpenter. The idea's ridiculous! I'm perfectly
capable of— If you'll just stop talking and hold the
ladder . . . and hand me the hammer . . . and
another nail. Keep still, Delia. Keep still! There now.
(*He brings down the hammer, then lets out a wild
wail.*) Ouch! Ou—ch! My thumb! My *thumb!*

OPEN HOUSE

SCENE: *Any ranch in Southern California, on any summer Sunday afternoon.*

(MRS. HILLIARD *speaks, she is wearing a large, floppy garden hat and several spangled bracelets.*)

There now, I think everything's ready. Punch. Cookies. Sandwiches. Flowers. Look, Allie, look at those trees! Did you ever see anything so heavenly? When I think of you and poor John living in that awful apartment, while Larry and I have the heavenly peace and quiet of this ranch. . . . Oh, Jennie, Jennie, have you scattered the ant powder? Good. And the netting covers for the wasps? Do tell Hannah to try and keep Heinie and Putzie— Oh, that reminds me!

Larry—Larry—Larr-i-bee! Jennie, have you seen Mr. Hilliard? With the pigs? Why should he be down with those revolting—

Oh, there you are, Larry. What on earth were you— Oh, you were? Well, it doesn't do the least bit of good. Tim Flitted them three times yesterday, and it just sent all the flies right up here.

And speaking of Tim, can't you lure him away

from the front drive? He looks so . . . well, so
. . . you know. . . .

The troubles I've had, Allie! We tried Japs . . .
I made them wear those Chinese pagoda hats, and
they looked adorable. Then we tried Mexicans in
sombreros—but Mr. Johnson, he's our foreman, in-
sists upon keeping Tim . . . just because he really
works. And you see how he looks! Without a shirt,
and wearing shorts. Why, everyone takes him for one
of the guests.

Leo! Leo! Drop that! Drop it, I say! Larry, yell
at him! It's my knitting! Oh, Jennie! Hannah! Catch
Leo!

There, I knew it! He's raveled the whole thing
out. Well, I'm sure I had to put it somewhere, Larry.
After all, I live here. If I'm getting in the way of
your Great Danes. . . . I'm sorry. Yes, Leo, yes, he
was a sweet dog, he was. Down, sir! Down! No,
Heinie, don't you start! Call Putzie! Please, Jennie,
call Heinie and Putzie . . . they're ruining my
dress.

There, Allie, let that be a lesson to you. When you
get a ranch— Oh, yes you will, dear—don't let John
have more than two dogs. And no monkeys! No matter what he tells you, no-o-o monkeys.

What's that, Jennie? Yes, I think five gallons will
be enough—to start with. You can brew more later
if— Larry! Larry, give Jennie the sherry for the
punch. Allie, if you and John want anything stronger

than punch, you'd better take it now. We don't dare serve it. They'd *never* go home!

I hope they don't run in too many mothers and grandmothers to-day. Yes, I love old people, really I do. Nice, white-haired old ladies sitting under the trees look sweet. Only, so few of them are white-haired . . . and they won't sit! Keep tearing around, wanting to play badminton, and filling up the swimming pool—and they never drown. No such luck. . . .

And the children—brats . . . and relatives from the East. . .

What? But, my dear, what a grotesque idea! Why, we love company. Really, we do. We look forward all week to Sunday. I tell everyone we keep open house—and send them all maps.

And it's good business, too. Lots of times Larry talks to people and sells them stories. Take to-day. There's a man coming—a Mr. Mackprang.

What's that, Jennie? He *did?* A whole plateful? *Two* plates? Larry! Larry! Leo's eaten a whole plate of sandwiches and one of cookies and was sick on the west patio.

That ends it! Tim! *Tim!* Will you please shut Leo up? Yes, with the Afghan . . . no, you can leave the dachs. They're all right if you keep 'em out of the pool. I'll never forget Putzie last week. Splash, and right in the Countess's lap! And the monkeys—

Oh, there comes the first load! Who is it? I don't

seem to recognize . . . but then lots of times I don't . . . they're just friends of friends, or it's the wrong ranch. Jennie! Hannah! They're beginning. You can put in the ice. Larry! Larry! They're beginning. Yes—no—thank goodness, they're passing by. It's all right, Larry. They're passing by.

What's that, dear? Hush, Heinie! I can't hear. Hush, Putzie! Why, yes, dear, of course I remember. The name is Mackprang. I'm sure I wouldn't be likely to forget that. Yes . . . and he owns five magazines. Imagine, Allie. Five! Do you suppose he reads all of 'em? I *am* sticking to the subject, Larry. You don't need to keep telling me! Don't I always?

Well, I couldn't help it that time. You remember what that Sunday was like. Allie, if you've ever seen a fire sale . . . Half of Hollywood, I give you my word . . . and the Historical Society backing into the pool. Yes, in a bus. They came to look at the house. It's all adobe, you know . . . and a hundred years old.

Listen, Larry—when this Mackprang person comes, I'll signal, and you'd better be around so I *can* signal. I couldn't last time. Oh, yes, you were, dear! With that red-headed Benson girl. I signaled and signaled. I did everything but hang by my knees. Well, you certainly couldn't expect me to swim out in the middle of the pool and bite you!

What, Hannah? The ice box? Oh, good heavens, Larry—it's the ice box again. It would choose to-day! Call the electrician. Yes, I know it's Sunday, but he lives just down the road. Hurry, Hannah. Hurry . . . tell him we'll pay double. . . .

Larry, will you pu-lease listen? When that Mackprang man shows up, you can take him down to the secret garden. Yes, it's all right—Tim took out the alligator. It's in with the geese . . . and, for heaven's sake, try not to look as though you were sneaking him off for a drink or you'll be doing the Pied Piper in no time.

Down, Mitzi, down! Bad kitty! Get off that table! Get! Never have a Siamese cat, Allie.

Oh . . . here's a car. The Tollivers. Wouldn't you know they'd come first? And loaded to the gunnels with relatives!

Oh, hello! Hello! How lovely to see you! Allie, you know Jane Tolliver . . . and William. Your cousins? From Philadelphia? How lovely! So glad you brought them! Mr. and Mrs. Smith . . . and little Rupert . . . and Sally. Delighted! Yes, delighted!

Yes, it's all adobe . . . built by the Indians . . . over a hundred years old. Yes . . . they're eucalyptus . . . twenty-seven feet around the base. Yes, darling, those are monkeys. No, dear, we don't feed them in the daytime. Yes, they bite when you stick your finger in. No, we don't like to have little girls poke them with sticks . . . nor little boys, either. Wouldn't you like some punch?

No, Putzie! No! They're nice little children. And cookies? Oh, I'm so sorry! And all over mud! You'll find a bathroom there—second door to the left. . . .

Oh, Helen! And Edgar! I didn't hear you drive in. And your sister from Poughkeepsie. How lovely! And her husband . . . and his mother . . . and her aunt. How lovely! Yes, we're always so glad . . . delighted. Yes, adobe . . . by the Indians . . . over a hundred years . . . yes, eucalyptus . . . about twenty-seven feet. (*Whispering.*) The second door to the left. (*Aloud.*) Won't you have some punch?

Leo! Leo! Drop that! Who let that dog loose? Is it *your* hat? I'm so sorry! Allie, will you please ask Jennie to— Oh, there you are, Jennie. On the telephone? Oh, you got the message. "Mr. Sweeney can't come." Thank you. Sweeney . . . Sweeney. Do you know any Sweeney, Allie? Do you, Helen? Jane? It couldn't be the Prince, could it? The Georgian one? He had a lot of aliases—but, come to think of it, he's in jail. . . .

(*From here on a note of hysteria creeps into* MRS. HILLIARD's *voice. She grows more and more scattered, speaking to left and right, as though to different groups, but always with the same fixed smile.*)

Hello! Hello! Mrs. Bannister . . . and the Judge. How lovely! And your uncle . . . and your aunt. Oh, your *great*-aunt. Heavens, Allie, the great-aunts are beginning! Some punch? Yes, very old . . .

a hundred years . . . and all adobe . . . by the Indians . . . about a hundred and twenty-seven. (*Whispering.*) The second door to the left.

Allie. Allie, will you ask Jennie to bring more—another gallon—and cookies—there come two more cars—and if you see anyone who looks as though he might be named Mackprang and own five magazines—

Why, hello, Marriam . . . and Jimmy! When did you— Oh, you have? (*Sotto voce.*) Listen, Marriam, have you any idea who those people are? Yes, down there by the monkeys—the awful woman with the comedy hat, and the bald man in the checked suit. I'm certain I've never laid eyes on them . . . oh— your sister and her husband? From Florida? But, Marriam, of course I knew. . . . I was jonly hoking —honly jo—only joking! You know we're delighted. Perfectly delighted! (*Whispering.*) The second door on the left.

Jennie, do you see that man wandering around by the front gate? It must be the electrician. Go get him—quick—and take him to the kitchen. He's *got* to fix that ice box. . . .

What? Oh, no, darling, we can't let out the monkeys. Yes, they knock things over . . . and frighten people . . . and sometimes they bite.

Punch? Cookies? Yes, adobe . . . the Indians . . . a hundred and twent— What, Hannah? Mr. Sweeney *is* coming? But I thought you said— Oh, he called again? Well, I'm sure I don't know who. Try and find Mr. Hilliard . . . ask him if he knows a Mr. Sweeney. . . .

Why, Elaine! Albert! This is a surprise! And you brought the twins! How lovely! (*Whispering.*) Yes, the second door— (*Aloud.*) No, dear, we can't let out the monkeys. Yes, adobe . . . a hundred years— Mitzie! Mitzie! Stop it! Did she hurt you, darling? Well, kitties always claw when you pull their tails. . . .

(*She grows more and more hysterical.*)

Yes, Siamese. A hundred and twenty-seven feet around . . . the swimming pool is the second door . . . I mean, it was built by the Indians. Allie . . . Allie, go and find Larry. Tell him I'll *kill* him if he doesn't come and help . . . and tell him the Mackprang hasn't come yet.

Yes, Hannah? He says he doesn't know how to fix it? Fix what? Oh, of course, the ice box. But he's got to fix it! Lock him in with it! We must have ice!

Oh, how-do-you-do? So glad to see you. I'm afraid . . . Your face is perfectly familiar, but your name— Hinkle? Oh, of course, Mr. Hinkle. Everybody, this is Mr. Hinkle. Wha—what? The electrician? But then who— What— Oh, good grief! Hannah! Hannah! That man you took to the kitchen . . . to work on the ice box . . . what did he say his name— Mackprang! He's gone? Stop him! Stop him! Catch him at the gate, somebody!

What's that? Who's screaming? (*Going completely to pieces.*) Good gracious! How did they— How could they— Larry! Larry! Judge Bannister's great-aunt has broken loose and bitten the monkeys! I mean, Judge Bannister's broken loose and bitten his great-aunt. I mean— What, Jennie? Mr. Sweeney can't come? Mr. Sweeney *can't* come?

(*She begins to laugh wildly.*)

Mr. Sweeney! No! No! I don't know who he is! Maybe I'll never know—but I love him! I love him! I *love* that man!

BOY CRAZY

SCENE: *A corner near a high school.*

(PEGGY WILLIAMS *enters, breathless. She carries three or four school books on a leather strap and is eating candy from a paper bag.* PEGGY *speaks.*)

Linda! Linda! Oh, my dear, I've been chasing . . . and chasing . . . and cha— I—I'm all out of breath. Wait'll I . . . wait'll I get it back! There. Oh-h-h! Have a candy? They're caramel. Darling, I'm simply—well, I simply can't tell you! You wouldn't believe it! I give you my word, you simply wouldn't . . . not if I told you a thousand times . . . who I met . . . absolutely met. Right on Elm Street. I'm not lying . . . you simply wouldn't believe . . . and was I devistated!

Wait! I'll let you guess. Blue eyes . . . with yellow hair, kind of crinkly . . . and shoulders . . . you wouldn't believe! Absolutely. Wait till I swallow. Wha—Bill Harding? I should say *not*. Why should I get excited about a boy that's been right here in this town ever since he was born? This was—well, my dear, you'll simply just about fall down dead! It was— (*Suddenly gazing out.*) Look—there's the

60

new chemistry prof. Do you think he's good-looking?
I don't, either, but Daisy Medford does. She's going
to sign for his course. . . .

What? Oh, yes . . . I was telling you . . . who
I met. Donald Ellerby. Absolutely—*Donald Ellerby*.
You remember . . . of course you do . . . the one
who used to be in high school until they moved back
East. With glasses . . . and braces on his teeth. Yes,
"Runtie"—that's what they used to call him—
"Runtie" Ellerby. Well, he's visiting his—

You don't think that's exciting? My *dear!* That
shows you haven't *seen* him. Just wait until you *have.*
Why, Linda—he's in Yale. Absolutely! I wouldn't
lie to you. *Yale!*

Here, have another candy. And it isn't only that
. . . my dear, if I could only *tell* you. Braces off his
teeth . . . and he isn't wearing glasses . . . and,
and he—well, he's *that* tall! Absolutely! And *this*
broad, and he— (*She pokes* LINDA *with her elbow.*)
Don't look now, but do you see that boy passing?
That's Mattie Davis's cousin, and he always tries to
act like we'd been introduced. My dear, he simply
devistates me!

Did I what? Well, what do you think? After telling you what Donald looked like! My dear, you
wouldn't have believed . . . why, he has a roadster.
Not just second hand. A real streamline—red, with
black wheels. And the way he looked . . . and the
way he talked—was I devistated!

Oh, hello, Bill. (*She nods casually.*) No, we're not going your way. No, thanks, I can't stop for a soda. Linda and I—we . . . we've got a lot of things we're kind of talking over. Yes. Ta-ta! See you some more. . . .

Goodness gracious, wouldn't that simply *devistate* you? I mean Bill coming along right now when I— well, when I was waiting. . . . It would have ruined everything. Absolutely everything!

What? Well, I *am* telling you. I'm telling you just as fast as ever I— I think I'll wear my blue, wouldn't you? Or maybe the flowered chiffon? That's cool looking. Oh, no, I forgot, I spilled punch on it. It'll have to be the blue, unless mother—but I don't suppose she would. She bought me the blue just last month, and when I spilled punch on the chiffon she said— Have another candy? I guess he'll like blue. Men usually do. And coming from Yale—

(*She sees someone in the distance.*)

Hush! That's Tommy Trenton over there. And the Baxter twins. I want to see if they'll cross over when they see us. Just kind of smile. No . . . they didn't. Well, I don't care. I guess I got something better'n a lot of high school kids to run around with.

My dear, don't you understand *yet?* It's the country club dance. Yes. To-night. Well, no . . . Donald hasn't exactly asked me . . . that is, not exactly . . . but, my dear, you'll never believe the way he looked at me. I mean, when I sort of happened to mention they still had dances. I mean, when I said they were having one to-night. Yes. He—he looked simply devistated.

(*She looks down the street, as though* LINDA *has called her attention to someone.*)

What did you say? Who? Where? No, that isn't him! That's just the new clerk at Bird's. Yes. The shoe department. He's *married*. Anyway, Donald is a thousand times better looking. Ten thousand—and then there's the car. Yes, he's going to pick me up. At least . . . I mean . . . he didn't exactly say so, but he mentioned he'd be driving home this way— after he finished with his grandfather. And I figure that's when he intends to ask me to go to the dance with him.

Oh, hello, Daisy! Hello! My dear, I've the most thrilling news for you! You'll never believe! Never in the world! You'll be simply and completely devistated. Have a piece of— Oh shoot, it's all gone! Listen, *who* do you think's in town?

You did? Well, how'd you know? What's that, Linda? Yes—red, with black wheels. What? Where? I don't see. It is! Yes, it *is* Donald. Why, he's got someone with him. Daisy . . . it's your big sister. She *is*? To-night? When did he ask her? I see. . . . Oh, well, she's from Vassar and we—we're just high school. But I should think he'd hate to run around

with anyone as old as she is. Why, she's twenty-one.
. . . Twenty-two? Why, that's practically middle
aged!

(*She follows the passing car with yearning eyes,
then crumples the bag and throws it away.*)

I guess I'll just stroll down past the drug store.
Maybe Bill's still— (*She suddenly sees something,
her eyes brighten.*) Linda . . . Daisy, look! The
one in the red sweater. It's . . . no, it isn't . . .
yes, it *is!* Buck Hennessy. He's back from Harvard
—he's won his *letter.* He's waving to me. He's—
(*She waves frantically.*) Yoo-hoo, Buck! Yoo-hoo!
Wouldn't that simply devistate you? Yoo-hoo-o-o!
(*She hurries out, waving.*)

MOVIE MOTHER

SCENE: *The casting office of a motion picture studio.*

(GWENDOLYN'S *mother enters; she is leading a small girl by the hand. She is carrying a bag and wears a very determined hat. Her speech wavers between a cloying affectation of sweetness and her own natural sharp vulgarity.*)

Are you in charge of casting? Smile for the lady, Gwendolyn. Oh, you aren't? It's Mr. Harris? Never mind, Gwendolyn. Then it's Mr. Harris I want to see. Yes. About a part for my little girl, here. Tell him it's Mrs. Smith. Mrs. George Padelford Smith. My daughter's name is Gwendolyn— Oh, no, no! Not Gwendolyn Smith . . . Gwendolyn Dawn. Mustn't contradict, darling. It's *always* been Dawn. Just because mother says so.

I beg pardon, miss? No. No experience in pictures —yet. But I'm sure they have only to see her . . . why, everyone tells me she's simply made for the screen.

Gwendolyn, use your hankie.

She's a lovely toe dancer . . . and she taps . . . and does acrobatics . . . and— What's that, miss? The bench? Oh, thank you.

65

Come, Gwendolyn. There . . . isn't that lovely and comfy? I'm sorry, madam. I wasn't conscious of shoving. I'm not in the habit of shoving, and I'm sure I couldn't have hurt your child. Umph! I think she's just crying to attract attention.

Hush, Gwendolyn! You mustn't say horrid things like that to other little girls. Where ever did you learn— He did? Well, you certainly shan't play with him any more!

What's that? Yes, dear, they're all little motion picture actresses, just like you. Darling, you mustn't stick out your tongue! Because it isn't polite! Of course mother doesn't. Oh . . . but that was different, dear. He was a doctor. Well, because doctors are—doctors are—that's enough about that, Gwendolyn. We shan't talk about it any more.

Don't, dear . . . please don't keep sliding down like that; you muss the ruffles of your darling little dress, and you know how hard mother worked— Don't put your hands there, dear! You'll get them all dirty—after we took so long to tint the nails.

Gwendolyn, come away from that blind! You'll break the rope. No, it's not meant to climb up. It's called a Venetian blind. Yes . . . It's to see through. No . . . I'm sure I don't know why they call it a blind when you can see through it. What? Well, Venice is a place in Italy where they have water for streets and boats for buses. (*To another mother.*) She's so bright and inquiring.

Gwendolyn, stop playing with that typewriter! Do you hear me? Stop it this minute! What, miss? But she couldn't have broken it . . . just looking at it. I'm sure the ribbon was pulled out before we came in. Well, I'm very sorry. Tell the lady you're sorry, Gwendolyn. Why of course you're sorry! Gwendolyn, if you ever say such a thing again, mother will take a big stick and—I mean, darling, mother's going to be very much annoyed, very.

What's that, miss? Oh, right away? Come, Gwendolyn. No, madam, it is *not* because she wants to get rid of us! Such rudeness!

Through this door, miss? Thank you. Now which gentleman? With the boil on his nose? Oh, yes. Wait a minute, darling. Let mother fix your curls. (*Sotto voce.*) Listen, Gwendolyn, if you say one single word about Mr. Harris's nose, I'll—don't ask why . . . mother's *telling* you!

Yes, miss, we're coming. Here, take mother's hand, darling. That's right.

(*She moves across the room.*)

Oh, good-morning, Mr. Harris. I'm Mrs. Smith, and this is Gwendolyn—Gwendolyn Dawn. Curtsey for the gentleman, darling, and remember what mama said! Never mind about what—just remember!

Mr. Harris, I know you must have a great many children brought to you, but Gwendolyn is different. Oh, in a great many ways! Everyone always says she is simply made for the screen. What? But, of course, she isn't cross-eyed! Oh, that—that's just when she looks at something terribly hard—she sort of—stop looking like that! Gwendolyn, mother says stop it!

Oh, yes, I should say so! Ye-e-es. She tap dances, and sings, and recites, and does acrobatics. Do a back-bend for the gentleman, Gwendolyn. O-o-opps! She's been in the Kulver Skool for Klever Kiddies two months now, and they say they've never seen a child with so much— Gwendolyn, stop playing with that blind! No, you can't pull the ropes!

I beg your pardon? Oh, yes, she learns things very quickly. She can recite—oh, all sorts of things. Gwendolyn, recite for the gentleman.

Of course, darling, you can look at him, if you're reciting. You'll *have* to look at him. Oh, you don't want to look at him? No, Gwendolyn, mother doesn't want to know why! (*Growing slightly fluttery.*) Because she *knows*—I mean—because she doesn't— Never mind about that; now just go ahead and recite.

Come! Come! "Little Miss Muffet—" That's right, dear. Yes. "Sat on a—" Now what did she sit on? No, Gwendolyn, *no!* She sat on a tuffet. Mother doesn't know what a tuffet is, darling—but that's what she was sitting on. And what was she doing? Yes . . . "Eating her curds and—" No, dear, not "*whee,*" "*whey.*" And what came along? Yes, you do, dear. Of course you do. You know, one of those

horrid creepy things with lots and lots of legs! No—
not a centerpiece. Oh—oh, isn't that cute? Did you
hear what she said? Centerpiece! She means centi-
pede. But it wasn't, darling, it was a—

Please, dear, please! Now put the gentleman's
glasses back on the desk. Do as I say! And don't do
that, dear—use your handkerchief!

Oh—dear—never mind! She just doesn't seem in
the mood to recite this morning. But isn't it wonderful to have such temperament at her age?

Gwendolyn, *put down* those glasses. Put them
down! Now look what you've done! Mr. Harris, I'm
so sorry! But I'm sure the child didn't deliberately
break your glasses!

But, of course, I'll be only too glad to pay for
them. You can deduct it from the very first pay check
for the very first picture you cast Gwendolyn in.

You will? There, Gwendolyn, the nice gentleman is
going to give you a part right away! Will there be
much to learn? Wha-a-at? Nothing? A hundred and
fifty other hoodlums? *Other!* Why, I—I—I never
was so insulted! How are people back home going to
know which is *my* child? Oh . . . well . . . I suppose every great artist has to start *somewhere*. Seven
o'clock? Yes, we'll be there.

Come, Gwendolyn—come.

PERFECT FORTY-TWO

SCENE: *The corset salon of a large department store.*

(MRS. C. WALTER PFAFF, *wearing a fur piece and armed with an umbrella, approaches the counter and tries to attract the attention of a clerk.*)

Pardon me, but are you— Pardon me, but are you— I beg your pardon, but are you busy? Oh, you are? Well, you just seemed to be standing around. . . .

Why, Mrs. Ross—think of meeting you! (*Over her shoulder.*) That's my umbrella. Your dress? I'm so sorry . . . but it's easy to mend. (*To* MRS. ROSS.) What are you doing here? Buying a corset! Well, well—isn't it a small world? (*Over counter to clerk.*) I want a corselette, size forty-two. (*To* MRS. ROSS.) Oh, she was waiting on you? I'm sure I had no idea . . . it's just that I'm in such a hurry. . . . We're leaving for California. Charlie and I. To-morrow. (*Over counter.*) I'm in a hurry, Miss. A dreadful hurry, because I'm leaving for California. What? Oh, didn't I? I was sure— I suppose it must have been some other clerk. A corselette. No, not a corset. I *never* wear a corset. A corselette is what I want. Size forty-two. (*To* Mrs. Ross.) I wouldn't mind shopping if it weren't for the clerks. (*To* Clerk.) I've been wearing the Dainty Maid, but I don't want that again—it shrinks so. (*To* Mrs. Ross.) You just wouldn't believe . . . every time I put it on it's smaller. (*To* Clerk.) Of course not! That's ridiculous. If I were gaining weight I'd be the first to notice it, wouldn't I? (*To* Mrs. Ross.) Idiots —all of them! (*To* Clerk.) No, I haven't lately— because the bathroom scales are broken. But if you'll just stop arguing and bring me what I asked for— (*To* Mrs. Ross.) Absolute idiots! (*Over counter.*) Oh, didn't I? Well, I'm sure I thought I'd made it perfectly clear. (*To* Mrs. Ross, *as she takes back her purse.*) Oh, did I drop my purse? Thank you. Dear me, and I had my ticket in it, too! My husband kept his. Wouldn't it have been funny if some woman had stolen this and used the ticket . . . it's a draw- ing room . . . and Charlie . . . can't you just *see* his face? (*To* Clerk.) Please, would you mind hurry- ing just a *little?* I've explained what a rush—

Well, I'm sure I thought I told you. I don't want a Dainty Maid—because of the shrinking. I want some- thing I saw on a friend of mine last week. (*To* Mrs. Ross.) Mary Kemble. Have you seen her lately? The way she's putting it on! It's disgus— (*To* Clerk.) No, that isn't what I want at all! There's no use trying to palm off imitations on me. I want ex- actly what I asked for!

What? Oh, I didn't? Why, of course I did. It— (*To* Mrs. Ross.) Now isn't that ridiculous? I've got it at the tip of my tongue. Right on the tip of— (*To the other side.*) Pardon me, madam, but you've dropped your fur. Why—it isn't yours, is it? It's mine! (*To* Clerk.) Let me see . . . I know it begins with an N . . . and it had a figure in it somewhere. No, not a number. A figure. You know—your figure . . . and it seems to me there was a girl in it . . . a young girl. Would it have been Virgin Shape? No, that doesn't sound right, does it? Maiden—that's it! I said it started with an M, didn't I? Maiden Figure . . . no . . . Maiden Shape . . . no . . . What? That's it! Fairy Form. I knew I'd remember!

Good gracious, my coat! I had it right over my arm. Somebody's stolen it! (*Calling.*) Floorwalker! Oh, Floorwalker! Oh, Floor— (*To* Mrs. Ross.) What? I didn't? Are you sure? Just the umbrella and my bag? Why no, of course, I remember now. I checked it. See . . . here's the ticket. (*To the* Clerk.) I checked it!

Oh, no, no, no! That isn't like the one I saw in the least. Not in the least! The one I'm talking about was pink, and it had lace at the top and— What's that one over there? It's a what? A Sally Slim? Have you size forty-two in that? Well, then, let me see it. (*She gives a little squeal and lifts her feet suddenly.*) Oh . . . what a shock! (*She picks up her fur.*) I thought it was a dog . . . and I simply can't stand

dogs. And how about the one over there? (*To*
MRS. ROSS.) Hairs all over the chairs . . . and always burying bones! (*To* CLERK.) Well, I don't like
it as well, but I might try it on. Where? Oh, all right.
(*To* MRS. ROSS.) Good-bye, my dear. It's been such a
joy to have this little visit. You'll excuse my going,
but I'm in such a hurry. . . .

Is this the room, Miss? I'm afraid you'll have to
close that window. It's drafty. Yes, very. (*Motions
of taking dress off over her head.*) Would you mind
giving a pull? It's just a trifle hard to . . . no-o-o
. . . it hasn't shrunk, but they sold me a thirty-eight
when I asked for a forty-two. I'm sure they did. You
know how some saleswomen are. Oh, it's my hat! I'll
have to . . . no . . . wait . . . you'll have to
. . . no . . . I will! (*Wild motions of getting a hat
and dress off at the same time, then emerging breathless.*) Just like a caterpillar! (*She takes a corset from
a salesgirl.*)

Now which is the front? Oh, it does? Well, the one
I've been wearing opens in the front. No, I'll do it
myself. (*Motions of stepping into the garment, then
going into a desperate struggle.*) But it won't pull
up . . . it isn't all unfastened . . . but it can't be!
Why, it's impossible for anyone— Listen, miss, I
can't *fight* my way into it! Of course I wear forty-two
. . . I've been a perfect forty-two for years. (*More
struggles.*) My last was a forty-two—the one that
shrank. (*Motions of stepping out.*) Never mind, I

don't like it anyway. All that fancy lace on the top
. . . and the garters. I don't like the garters at all.
They'd make bumps where I sit.

Here, let me try that other one. (*More motions of
getting into a garment.*) There . . . that's better
. . . lots better. What make did you say this one
was? (*She looks at the label.*) Why, it's a forty-four!
I can't possibly wear a forty-four. It would simply
hang off me in folds! What? Oh, it *is?* If you ask me,
I think they're very careless. You'd think a big firm
like that would stamp on the right sizes, wouldn't
you?

No, let me fasten it myself. I let a saleslady fasten
it one time—and then they wouldn't take it back.
Charlie—I mean, my husband—had to hook me up
for months. . . . (*Wild motions of reaching
around under her left arm.*) What did I tell you? It's
way around at the back! I'd practically have to be
a contortionist. . . . I'd have to stand on my head!
And, anyway, the hooks are too large. They dig in.
Couldn't we have a window open? It's frightfully
stuffy . . . and a . . . a digging-in-hook is the last
thing I can bear—especially on a train trip.

A what? You have? A zipper? That sounds perfectly lovely—why didn't you tell me instead of getting me into these things? Oh, you've brought one?
Well . . . let's see. . . . (*Motion of stepping into
the garment.*) There! This is more like it! The color
. . . and the boning . . . so it won't bag in front.

Bag. Bag! Good gracious, I've left it! My bag—out there somewhere. I think on the counter. Would you mind? It's got my railroad ticket . . . oh, blue alligator with a duck's head . . . and hurry! Please hurry! I'll get into this one while you're gone. . . .

(*She looks into the mirror, smiles, then reaches down on the left side and makes motions of grasping something between thumb and fingers.*)

A zipper! H'm-m . . . nice!

(*With a beaming smile, she gives a firm pull, from bottom to top. Her face twists into a wild expression.*)

Oh! Ouch! Oh, miss! Miss! Somebody—anybody —come quick! Help me! Help! I've zipped myself! I've zipped myself! Help!

BRAIN STORM

Scene: *A psychopathic ward.*

(*A* Prisoner *speaks.*)

It was this way, Doctor. We'd been married ten years. No, not quite ten . . . more like nine and five months. We got married in August. So's we could take in the State Realtors' Convention on our honeymoon. About the middle it was—the fifteenth or sixteenth—which makes it nine years and five months, less eight ⁀ nine days. Being accurate is a thing I can't help. That's what I used to tell her. Hundreds of times. Or I guess probably it was more like thousands.

"That's the way I was born, Ellie," I'd say. Her name was Elaine, but I called her Ellie. "No use getting mad about it. . . ."

Not that she ever really got mad. She wasn't the getting mad kind. Only, she would try to hurry me sometimes . . . about eating . . . or talking. Perhaps you notice I talk kind of slow. Not drawl . . . just slow, and careful. I'm like that about everything, you'll find out—if you take my case. I don't ever say anything, or do anything I haven't thought about . . . only that once. I didn't think about that. It just happened without my thinking. That's what makes it so—

Yes, I guess you're right, Doctor. I better start at the beginning. That's the way to tell a story. I used to tell that to Ellie when she said I started too far back.

"But you got to build up a story," I'd tell her. "You got to start at the beginning—even when it's only a funny anecdote."

Yes, Doctor, I'm coming to how it happened. I just wanted you to know a little about Ellie. How she was always a good wife—so's you can explain to the judge. I must have been crazy! Or had a brain storm, or whatever it is they call it. Ellie could tell you, because she reads. I mean, she used to read a lot about things like that—all about glands, and how people weren't to blame for what they did. Only, I didn't ever take any stock in that new-fangled stuff.

"Just coddling," that's what I used to tell her, "just coddling criminals and murderers."

I s'pose that sounds funny coming from me, now. Only, I'm not really a murderer, Doctor. Just a law-abiding citizen that's had a brain storm.

It wasn't as though I owned a gun. I had to borrow it. And when the police say that shows premeditation, they're crazy. I borrowed it from the fellow

in the apartment over us. I was kind of surprised he
was home, because when I found the note, the one
Ellie left, it flashed over me it might be him she went
with.

No, she didn't say anything about going with a
man. But of course I knew she'd gone with a man
. . . because women always *do,* and I was pretty
sure I knew where to find 'em.

We'd been motoring once, going to see my folks
upstate. Ellie didn't want to go much, but I made her.
Not made her exactly . . . but sort of persuaded her
—by asking her what she planned to use for money
while I was gone. Not that I was ever mean about
money. Used to joke about it.

"Where's the dollar I gave you last week?" I'd
say. Or sometimes I'd pretend to give her ten, and
then take it back and give her five. Just for fun.

Well, anyway, she went on the trip, and it was on
the way upstate. A sort of inn where we stopped to
ask the way when we got off the main road.

Ellie was crazy about it because it was full of old
furniture. She was always fussing about antiques
when we were first married. Wanted to buy some for
the apartment.

"What's the matter with Grand Rapids?" I used
to ask her. "What's the use buying old broken-down
things when you can get swell new stuff that matches
all up for half the price?"

Well, the lady owns the place let Ellie go upstairs

to see a bureau—or maybe it was a bed—that was up
there. When she came down, I said:

"You certainly stayed long enough."

"I'd like to stay here the rest of my life," she
told me.

"Well," I said, "then you wouldn't spend it
with me."

"No," she said. "Not with you."

Of course I laughed, but it stuck in my mind, some-
how. When I found that note, it all came back to me
. . . and I went right out and got into my car. Oh,
yes, that's right, first I borrowed the gun. Told the
man I was going on a night trip and was afraid of
holdups. He let me have it. He's always wanted to
get acquainted, but I never was very friendly . . .
didn't want him running in all the time.

"A man wants a place where he can take off his
coat and shoes and be comfortable while he reads the
sport sheet," I used to tell Ellie. "He don't want
people running in all the time."

Oh, yes, I was talking about that gun, wasn't I?

I didn't borrow it because I was mad, or because I
intended to shoot the fellow Ellie had gone off with.
I just wanted it so's to be able to show him I wasn't
going to stand for any funny business when she left
him to come back with me.

Of course I intended to take her back. Lots of men
wouldn't—after her running away with another fellow like that. . . . But I'm broad-minded.

I expected to be pretty cross for a while. Not sulky. I'm never sulky . . . but I guess everybody gets sharp sometimes when things don't go right. A man's got to be sharp sometimes or he gets put upon.

But I haven't a thing to reproach myself with. Not a thing. No woman ever got treated better than Ellie. And then she had to go and leave me. . . .

That's what I was telling you, wasn't it? About the way I got into the car and drove up to that place where we'd seen the old house?

Well, Ellie was there, all right. I knew, because I could see her coat hanging in the downstairs hall. I guessed she and her lover were upstairs, because there were lights in two rooms that opened out on to a porch.

I was still all right, Doctor. Cool as a cucumber. When I pulled out the gun from the car and went up some outside stairs to the porch, it wasn't with any idea of shooting . . . it was just to show the man I meant business, and to make him keep quiet—so's nobody but the three of us'd ever know.

Well, I walked right in on Ellie.

Funny I can talk like this about her, isn't it? I mean without getting worked up or anything. You'd think after what happened—

I can't realize she's dead! I can't! I can't!

No . . . no . . . I'm not getting excited. I'm just trying to explain how it was.

"Where is he?" I asked her. Not mad at all, Doctor, just "Where is he?"

She didn't answer at first . . . I saw she was thinking quick.

"Don't try to get out of it," I told her. "Is he there in the bedroom?"

"There isn't anyone in the bedroom," she told me.

I walked across and threw open the door. I give you my word, Doctor, I wouldn't have shot him. Not even then. Not even after her lying about it. I didn't have the thought of shooting in my mind. All I wanted was to call him out so's he'd see her go back with me. He'd have been as safe as a baby with me. Honest he would, Doctor. Safe as a baby—if I'd found him.

Only I didn't.

There wasn't anything in the bedroom except a bureau and a bed, that hadn't been slept in. And there wasn't another door. When I turned back Ellie was looking at me sort of funny . . . as though she was scared—no, not scared—as though she felt sorry for me.

"There isn't any man, Jim," she said. "Nobody had anything to do with my leaving you."

"You're lying!" I told her . . . only, I knew she wasn't lying. I knew.

"I didn't mean to tell you," she said, "but I've been writing for a long time. I've sold two stories. They want more. Now I can go away where I won't have to look at you—listen to you—ever again."

That's when I shot her. Right at that minute. Why, Doctor? *For God's sake, tell me why!*

I'M SURE I COULD WRITE

SCENE: *The reception room of a woman's club, just after a famous novelist has lectured.*

(MRS. PETER J. BLODGETT *speaks. She wears a hat of the dreadnaught type, and has a pair of tortoise shell glasses suspended on a wide ribbon around her neck. She is smiling and clapping her hands.*)

Lovely! Lovely! Ye-e-es, wasn't it?

(*She takes one or two little running steps and intercepts someone.*)

Oh, Miss Hathaway—I'm Mrs. Blodgett. Yes, Mrs. Peter J. Blodgett, Chairman of the Fine Arts Section. I just had to come and shake your hand and tell you how thrilled, absolutely thir-r-rilled, I was with your talk. It was an inspiration. Oh, yes it was, my dear! An absolute inspiration! And just simply inspiring.

I'm crazy about your books, too. Crazy. I go down on the waiting list at the library for them the very first moment I hear they're out. Why, if I'd only known you were going to talk to-day, I'd have bought one for you to autograph.

But I got the date mixed. I thought you were going to be James Hilton. I mean I thought James Hilton—well, you know what I mean. So I made a special effort to get here. Missed a bridge luncheon. Wasn't that a joke on me?

Oh, dear . . . look the other way . . . or, wait . . . turn your back! It's Mrs. Hornbeck, our Vice President. She's the most dreadful woman . . . hasn't a good word for anybody, and she'll simply freeze on to you. . . . (*Speaking to* MRS. HORNBECK.) Hello, dear. How perfectly sweet you look! Isn't that a new dress? Oh, really? Well, the bow is new anyway. I'm just taking Miss Hathaway in to get some tea. Yes, wasn't it? Simply inspiring! (*To* MISS HATHAWAY.) There, I got rid of her for you . . . but she'll be back. She's that kind. Always chasing lions. Why, she's asked James Hilton to stay at her house. Imagine! (*Grasping her arm.*) I suppose I'd better take you in for tea since I said I was going to. Of course, we'll all have to go to her house if we hope to meet him. And I'm crazy about his books. Crazy. Especially—what's its name?—you know, the one about the fireman. Only, there isn't a fireman in it.

What? But I'm sure there was some mention of a fireman, something about ringing a bell. Wait a minute! Wait a minute! I have it! "The Postman Always Rings Twice." I knew there was a bell in it! James Hilton didn't write it? Then who— James what? James Cain . . . of course! I knew that just as well as I know your name, Miss Holloway—I mean, Miss Hathaway.

Wait! Do you mind stepping in here? It's just the cleaning closet . . . but there're several women out there waiting to nab you— Annabelle Parkinson's one of them. Peek out and you'll see her. Yes, the one with the hat like an ice-bag. I want to warn you— she'll pretend she's read every one of your books and she won't have read a line of any of them. Not a *line*. Only the review in the newspaper. She takes the New York Herald Book Section just to save her from reading anything.

Listen, wouldn't it be fun to stay in here a little while? It's sort of cozy, don't you think? You can take that chair. No, I guess you better not . . . it's got a broken back. I suppose that's why they've put it in here. I'll take it. You can sit there on the step-ladder—and we'll talk about your books.

Oh, I'm so sorry! It's just the dust mop. It didn't hurt your hat, really. Give it to me and I'll brush it off. What I say is, the only thing that counts with authors is a good long talk . . . all about their books. Which one of your books do I like best? Well . . . now . . . let me think. . . . I can't say about the last one because I haven't quite got around to reading it yet. And the one before that I didn't get clear through, because the woman I borrowed it from left town. But I saw the picture they made out of the one before that. I was simply crazy about it! Crazy. Es-

pecially the place where the airplane crashes in
Samoa and the girl has to go native.

Oh, there wasn't? Why, Miss Hallowell—I mean
Hathaway—I was certain you wrote that. You're
sure you didn't? I mean, the movies change things so.
Well, of course—anyway—I was crazy about it—
yes. Crazy.

No, you don't have to go out there yet. All those
women want to do is nab you and shake your hand—
just so they can brag about it. I always say it doesn't
mean a thing . . . just shaking somebody's hand.
My grandfather shook P. T. Barnum's hand, and
what good did it do him?

I suppose you'll hardly believe this, Miss Hathaway . . . but I have the strangest feeling sometimes. Absolutely the strangest! I've had it ever since
I was a little girl. You know, *I'm sure I could write.*

Dear me, I haven't dusted off your hat yet!

I can't begin to tell you the ideas I have, Miss
Hathaway! (*She begins to dust the hat, but it soon
lies in her lap, forgotten.*) You won't believe me!
And the plots! Whole, long plots—all ready to put
down . . . if I could just find the time. They'd make
my fortune. All those big beautiful plots rolling over
and over in my head begging to be let out! If only
someone would help a little . . . like letting me tell
them my ideas and putting them down on paper. I'd
be only too glad to let the other person keep half of
what she got for them. Only not for the movie rights,

of course . . . because all she'd have to do would be
the writing—and then sell them.

Maybe you know somebody who would like to do
something like that. You don't? Well . . . maybe
you'd like to do it yourself. Oh, you are? Well . . .
then, I'll tell you . . . if I manage to get time to
write them down myself, I'll just send them on to
you. Yes, and you can sort of look them over and tell
me what you think. Of course I wouldn't mind a bit
if you showed them to your editors. If you'll give me
your address— Oh, you are? Around the world? You
don't know *how* long you'll be gone? Well, when you
get back, just drop me a line. (*To someone coming
in the door.*) Oh, my dear—were you looking for us?
Well, I'm terribly sorry, but we had a lot to talk over
—yes. Miss Hallworthy—I mean Miss Hathaway
—was just trying to persuade me to do a little writing
with her. Yes. (*To* MISS HATHAWAY.) It's been
such an inspiration meeting you, my dear—to have a
little talk with another author—in this mental des-
ert. Such an inspiration!

Good-bye! Good-bye! Oh . . . you forgot your
hat! Miss Hallworthy—I mean Miss Hathaway—
your hat. Your hat. Miss Hathaway—your hat!

(*She exits hurriedly, waving the famous novelist's
hat in the air.*)

THREE-MINUTE TALK

SCENE: *The banquet room of a Midland hotel.*

(*Having been introduced by the chairman,* MR.
PETER K. DUMBRODIE *rises to his feet. He bows to
left and right, clears his throat, arranges a glass of
water on the table in front of him, clears his throat
again, and begins.*)

Boys . . . I mean—er—gentlemen. (*He pulls
down his vest, arranges his tie, clears his throat and
goes on.*) When Bill—I mean when Mr. Busworth—
said he had put me on the program to-night I—uh—
I—uh—told him I wasn't—I mean isn't—I mean
amn't a speaker . . . not *any* kind of a speaker. I
said, "Hell, Bill, I can't—" I mean I said, "Honestly,
Mr. Busworth, I can't talk for ten minutes. I can't
talk for even five minutes." So Bill said—so *he* said
—it'd be all right if I only talked for one minute
. . . just so long as I told you all something about
—uh—something about business conditions in the
West.

(*He starts to put his thumbs in the armholes of
his vest, thinks better of it, and puts his hands in his*
88

*pockets, thinks better of that, and puts them down on
the table.*)

I guess Bill—uh—Mr. Busworth thought I ought
to know about business conditions in the West, because I've just come from . . . from a two-three
weeks trip to the Coast, and if it'll help you guys—
uh—you gentlemen any, I'll be only too glad to hand
you any tips—uh—to give you any information I can.

(*He suddenly begins to suspect that the front of
his shirt is gaping, investigates, shoves it together,
and again pulls down his vest.*)

Well . . . business conditions in the West—well
—uh—you might say they're just about like business
conditions in the East. In some places they're more
so. In some places they're—well—uh—you might
say they're less. That is where there *were* any business conditions . . . because in some places I
stopped—like where there are strikes—there just
aren't any . . . any business conditions, I mean.
(*He pulls down his vest again.*)

But they're looking for things to get better right
along! That is, if the strikes don't go on . . . in
which case, they'll get worse.

(*He takes a swallow of water, manages to spill
some down his front, brings out a handkerchief,
wipes his shirt front, then mops his brow, and con-
tinues, with an agonized expression.*)

Now Bill—Mr. Busworth—said I was to tell you
about—uh—about any little thing I'd heard that

might be amusing. Like a funny story. Well, I—uh—
I didn't do much traveling in Pullmans. That is, I
drove in my car. And nights I was mostly too tired
to get around. Besides, my wife was along.

But one fellow . . . he was in tinwear. I met him
in Seattle. Moffitt, his name was. I forget the first
name—anyway—he was in tinware. He told me a
yarn that maybe—uh—well, maybe it'll—well, anyway, it seems like there was a Dutchman and an Irishman . . . and they were married on the same day.
I mean, they were married to their wives on the same
day.

Anyway, the Irishman met the Dutchman and he
said, "Sure an' tomorrow's our anniversary, Adolph,
an' phat are you gettin' your wife?" And the Dutchman, he said to the Irishman, "Begorrah, Pat—" No
. . . he said, "Ach Himmel! Vot vass I gettin' my
vife, iss it?" and the Irishman said, "Begorrah, dot
vass vot I—" I mean he said, "Mein Gott, that was
what I—" No, I mean he said— (*Completely con-
fused and sunk in embarrassment.*) Well, anyway, it
was a swell story!

And now I see three minutes is up . . . and I was
only going to . . . to talk one minute. But when I
get to talking about business conditions in the West
I get kind of carried away and I—uh—I hope some
of you guys—gentlemen—will—uh—will—uh—find
what I have said useful to you in your—uh—in your
business contacts, and that when you go West you—

you'll find business conditions just like I said . . . only more so, if you get what I mean. Goodnight! (*He sits down, still mopping his brow, and expells his breath in a long whistle of relief.*) Whew!

ROCKING CHAIRS

SCENE: *The front porch of a house in a small town.*

(MRS. CROOPER *speaks. She is a matron with broad features, and a large, untidy figure. She is fanning herself with a palm-leaf fan, and rocks incessantly.*)

Put it right down on the table, Martha. Hope y' got enough lemons in it this time. Spread a napkin over it. Flies is turrible. No . . . don't put the one with the hole in it! What would the neighbors think? There, that's better.

Scat! Scat! Martha, there she is up on the table again! Always snoopin' inta somethin'. I declare to goodness that cat's worse'n a nosey old woman! Take her along to the kitchen with you.

Oh, hello, Mr. Snyder! What say? Yes, awful hot. Don't seem to bother you none. Never seen y' lookin' so spry. On your way down to the post office, I s'pose? Well, the mail won't be sorted out yet. They get slower down there ev'ry day—'specially now the vacation post cards have started comin' in.

How's Mrs. Snyder's cold? Yes, a summer cold is about the provokin'est thing I can think of. Dangerous, too. Mrs. Parker started with just one of those aggravatin' summer colds. A week later she was flat on her back with pneumonia. Three days later she was—well, you went to the fun'ral.

What say? Mebbe . . . but even if the doctor says she is better 'tain't no sign she *is*. Those doctors don't know as much as they think they do. All they want to do is operate . . . operate . . . cut you open—an' half the time in the wrong place.

Scat! Scat! What say? No, I was just yellin' at the cat . . . Martha's gone and let her out again.

Good-bye! (*Calling after him.*) Now you tell your wife to take care of herself, or first thing she knows she'll be layin' right alongside poor Mrs. Parker.

Oh, hello, Mrs. Jacobson. Yes, awful hot. My goodness, you look all tuckered out. You ought to know better'n be hurryin' in this heat—a woman your age. And you hadn't ought to be carryin' a big package like that.

What say? Well, it *looks* heavy. It's a what? Now what in the world y' carryin' a rag bath mat around the streets for? Oh, yes . . . I clean forgot all about the Church Fair bein' to-day! Why didn't Mr. Jacobson take you over in the car? Oh, he is? Well, I don't see any sense of his goin' 'way out to the Kradle place on a day like this.

What say? Yes, I s'pose, heat or no heat, business is business, an' bankers is about the only ones that have any now-a-days.

Oh, have you got to go? I certainly hope you make lots of money on that rug of yours. But then I don't guess anybody's payin' much for rags sewed up into bath mats in these times. What say? Yes, I may be down when it cools off a mite. I got some washrags for 'em. An' some calico pot-holders. Good-bye. 'Bye.

Hello, Susy! What say? Yes, mighty hot. Better come on up here and set a spell. Oh, it won't be sorted out yet. Mr. Snyder just went past. He allus goes down early . . . then stands around gabbin' and agabbin'. I allus say old men are twice as gossipy as women.

Take the green chair, there. That's better. Nothin' like a good old-fashioned rocker for solid comfort . . . kinda keeps a body's mind active, too.

Help yourself to some lemonade. Martha just made it up fresh. The sun's hittin' your back. Better slew your chair a mite to the left. There.

What say? Oh, I thought you said somethin'. You ain't snifflin', are y', Susy? Them pesky summer colds is the worst kind. Look at Mrs. Snyder. Wh—at? You mean t' say y' ain't heard? Down flat on her back with pneumonia. Poor soul, they don't know yet whether she'll pull through or not. Doctor was up with her all night long. Mr. Snyder was tellin' me all about it, just 'fore you come by. Poor man, he looked like death itself.

Scat! Reach back, Susy, an' push that cat off the table.

Oh, hello! (*She waves her fan.*) Hello, Miss Kradle . . . Mrs. Trowbridge. Yes, it is a nice day, ain't it—'cept for the heat.

Well! Did you hear that? "Nice day." An' so hot a person can hardly breathe. I s'pose if y' could go sailin' past in an automobile, like some folks do, it would be a nice day. I guess they'll be singin' out of the other side of their mouth when the bank comes down on 'em. Oh, hadn't you heard? That place of theirn is mortgaged right up to the hilt. Wonder how their mother's goin' to feel when she gets back from galavantin' all over Europe and finds out she ain't even got a place to lay her hat. Where'd I hear what? Oh, nobody said anything. I just put two and two together. Mr. Jacobson from the First National ain't spendin' half his time up to their farm 'thout there's somethin' in the wind. He's up there right this minute.

What say? Oil? Well, well, I declare—is that a fact? Don't some people have all the luck? Glad they're goin' to get somethin' out of that old farm at last. Just hope they'll give what they ought toward the church debt . . . an' mebbe they will—but I doubt it.

I allus say charity starts at home. What say? I mean if that new preacher is so good at talkin' people out of hell he ought to begin by talkin' the church out of debt.

Scat! Drat that pesky cat!

I know he's only been here a week. He may be a good enough preacher, but what do any of us know about him? Come from Salt Lake, an' that's about all we know so far. That's the place all them Mormons are at. I ain't never seen one that I know of— but from all I hear, y' can't trust 'em as far as you can see when it comes to women.

'Course I know his wife came with him! *This* wife did. But how's a body to know how many more of 'em he's got back in Salt Lake?

What say? How do *you* know they only marry one at a time now-a-days? Well . . . mebbe so . . . an' mebbe not. But y' can't never tell where a man like that is goin' to break out. It's in the blood.

Help yourself to some more lemonade there. That's right.

What d' you hear from Effie? Oh, she is? Well, once she gets here, mark my words, she'll stay more'n two weeks! I guess she's like all the rest of the girls . . . one little spat an' they come runnin' home to mother. What say? Happy with him? Well, I don't s'pose she'd tell you if she wasn't. Seems like her mother is about the last person on earth a girl tells her troubles to these days. Why, Sarah Jane Bixby was clear divorced before her mother even heard about it.

What say? Well, if you must go, I s'pose you must. They ought to have the first-class mail about sorted by this time. Glad you stopped by.

Oh, don't mention it! I'll tell Martha what y' said
. . . yes, she always likes to hear that people rel-
ished her lemonade. Cooks are like that. Good-bye
. . . good-bye. If y' get a letter from her, let me
know when your daughter's arrivin'. Good-bye. . . .

Shoo! Shoo-o-o!

Martha! Mar—tha! Better come an' take that
lemonade in. It's drawin' the flies somethin' turrible!
What'd you do, ferget t' put the sugar in it again?
Susy Gordon stopped by for a minute . . . she
couldn't hardly drink the stuff it was so sour. What
if her glass is empty? She had to be polite, didn't she?
Poor soul, she's certainly havin' a peck of troubles!
Couldn't hardly keep back the tears. She just got a
letter from that daughter of hern. Comin' home
again—bag 'n' baggage. I allus said I wouldn't give
that marriage a year—an' I was right!

When you get rid of that tray, fetch me my liver
pills . . . don't slam the screen door like that!

Oh, never mind about the pills . . . never mind.
I'll get 'em my ownself. I want to put on my hat and
go down to the Church Fair—see if anythin' has been
happin' lately. Jus' sittin' here on the front porch,
half the town might be dead an' I wouldn't know
about it.

(*She sighs and goes into the house.*)

CALORIES

SCENE: *A weight-reducing room in Madame Arlen's beauty-salon.*

(RUBY McGUIRE *speaks. She is wearing a tight gym cap and has a towel around her neck.*)

Oh, there you are, Mrs. Sessions! I was kind of beginning to think you'd forgot this was Thursday. Well, that's too bad—but with the traffic like it is, the best way is just to start the five minutes ahead you're going to be late, if you get what I mean.

Will you step on the scales, please? Well! Well! Four pounds off. No—wait. You're scroochin' over so it don't all register. There, that's better.

Why, Mrs. Sessions! Shame on you! You've put on a pound and a half! I knew the minute I laid eyes on you. I said to myself, "She's tryin' to hide it by pullin' her breath, but she's been eatin' again." It just kind of stuck out all over you. (*She indicates where it sticks out.*)

Yes, I know it's awful—smellin' the food, and all. But I tell my ladies if they'll just chew gum . . . real hard . . . like this . . . see? . . . for five

minutes right before they sit down to a dinner party
. . . or eat a raw onion, with salt . . . you'd be
surprised!

Now I'll start the music and we'll do the new exercise. (*Movement of starting a phonograph.*) The
bend-and-swing—with a push at the end. Remember?
Bend, swing around—hindside before—sort of like a
pretzel, then push. See? *Push*. Now you try. Bend,
one-two. Swing, one-two. Pu-s-sh, one-two. Keep it
up. . . .

I saw your pitcher in the paper the other day, Mrs.
Sessions. Yes . . . the club-lady one. Push, Mrs.
Sessions . . . push hard! Funny, I wouldn't of seen
it only my husband— Why, yes, I'm married. Didn't
I tell you? That is, I'm kind of married. He's a
traveling salesman. (*She laughs.*) That's one of
Hank's jokes. He's a card! A regular card! Now
we'll do the crawl-on-the-floor one. Yes, with your
hands behind you—like a worm. That's it!

You'd of died if you heard what Hank—that's my
husband—said about the pitcher. Honest, you'd of
split laughin'. Not so much what he said—the way he
said it. You aren't humpin' enough, Mrs. Sessions.
Think about a caterpillar and hump in the middle.
That's the ticket!

Well, Hank said . . . he was eatin' bacon and
eggs, for breakfast, at the time . . . that's what
made it so screamin' . . . he handed over the paper
with the pitcher and said—hump up . . . up—he

said, *"There's* a lot of hawgs would make good bacon."

Why, no, Mrs. Sessions! He didn't mean *you*. Lots of the club ladies in that pitcher were fatter'n you. The one sittin' on the table in the organdie dress . . . she was a regular hippopot— Your sister? Well, well! It certainly runs in the family, don't it?

Did you read about Mrs. Harlan's divorce? Yes, I felt real bad. She used to be one of my ladies, but she stopped comin'. And lemme tell you, Mrs. Sessions, that's where she made a terrible mistake. If she'd come in regular—not every now and then, the way you do—but regular, and taken the whole course, she'd never have lost him.

All right. Now we'll do the swing-the-hips. One-two. One-two. One-two . . . I don't know whether you've noticed, Mrs. Sessions, but the ladies that have sort of put it on, is the ones that's always losin' their husbands.

Why, no, Mrs. Sessions, I wasn't insinuatin'. Everybody knows how devoted Mr. Sessions is to you. Why, only yest'day a lady that knows you real well was sayin' she simply couldn't understand it— it was the wonder of the age how he stuck.

And such a good-lookin' man, too. Sure, I've seen him. Somebody pointed him out the other day. He was havin' lunch with your daughter—you sure have a pretty girl, Mrs. Sessions. Oh, you haven't? Well,

I guess I must of been mistaken. He probably just happened to stop and speak to the lady. What? Well, I didn't look close—but she was young and slim . . . an' had red hair.

Oh, his secretary. Well, then, it was just business. Anyways, *you* don't need to worry, Mrs. Sessions, with him so devoted to you and all. . . .

Tired? You do look kind of pale. We'll do some mat work. That's right. Flat. Real flat. Now raise the right leg over the head until it touches the wall . . . bring the left leg up beside it . . . kind of rest on your elbows and jiggle up and down on your shoulder blades. Now again . . . again . . .

I never see anyone do that jiggle exercise I don't think of Mrs. Lovett. Yes, Mrs. John G. Lovett. Didn't you know she was one of my ladies? Well, she was—many's the time she's laid right on that mat where you're layin' an cried so hard she couldn't hardly put her foot over her head.

Yes . . . the papers got it just about right, except that the girl who took her husband wasn't in the chorus. She was a manicurist. Um-hmm . . . from the barber shop downstairs.

You can slack off now, and we'll do the steam cabinet. There. Stretch out . . . and relax. Relax! Relax! That's better. Want an ice bag? All right, I'll stand here and fan you.

Married fifteen years. Mr. and Mrs. Lovett was,

I mean. I'd like to split first time she came in. She said she'd kind of let herself go and wanted to get back to her old weight. Imagine! She tipped the scales at a hundred and eighty-seven and wanted to get down to a hundred-five! Of course, it can be done, Mrs. Sessions, but not by her. Glandular. . . . Why, a mouse'd starve on what she ate.

Oh, are you? Lemme look at the thermometer. Pardon, my error! 'S a wonder you weren't boiled!

And exercise. If you'd seen her ridin' the rockin' horse and roll—say, she just about rolled a hole in the floor! Honest, you'd of died laughin'. What? Maybe you're right. Maybe it was kind of pitiful. But I got such a sense of humor.

Maybe we'd better get you a little ice, Mrs. Sessions. Your face is pretty red, an' we don't want any apoplexy. It always makes Madame sore as— Hey, Margie, will you bring some ice? Yeah, ice—*ice*. For Mrs. Sessions. Thanks . . . that's a pal!

I was just tellin' Mrs. Sessions, here, about Mrs. Lovett. She's real interested, seein' she's about the same weight, an' all.

Say . . . look at the time! I never noticed! You're five minutes overdone and ought to be in the violet right now. I got so interested. Here . . . lemme help you on to the table.

Sometimes I think if Mrs. Lovett had taken violet ray . . . but she thought she couldn't afford it. I guess by that time her husband was spendin' considerable on the blonde . . . and nothin' else did her any good. She'd sweat off a pound one day—maybe two in a week—then it'd come right back again.

There you are. Now relax while I fix the light.

Say, it's a funny thing, but this is the very room where Mrs. Lovett— Drat that cord, it's twisted again! Yea, right from that window there. You can see by the awnin' down below. They had to put in new canvas. Yeah, clean through it—right on to the sidewalk.

She'd just been weighin' in, an' she'd gone up two pounds. I only left her for a minute. . . . Turn over, will you, so I can work on your— That's right!

Funny what we women'll do if a man gives us the go-by. I know if Hank was to . . . an' you know how you'd feel if Mr. Sessions— Say, did I turn the light into your eyes? It makes 'em water, don't it? There, I've turned it off.

Now I'm goin' to tuck you in and leave you for your rest period, Mrs. Sessions. You're to think nothin' but happy thoughts! That's Madame's orders.

What? Sure, we're goin' to get you down to weight. Sure, you're goin' to look like a girl again. Just like a thin, beautiful girl. All you got to do is come regular, and take the whole course—violet ray 'n' all.

Now close your eyes. And remember—happy thoughts. . . .

(*She tiptoes away several feet, then speaks in a lower tone.*)

Hey, Margie, got a camel? Thanks. Speakin' of camels, I been workin' on that Sessions dame. Yeah, the one's husband is playin' around with the red-head. Maybe I didn't fix her to take the whole course! Maybe I didn't—with ten per cent comin' to me! Say, what'd you get, a hat or new shoes?

Who screamed? What's that noise? Why's that crowd down there? Mrs. Sessions? No, she didn't! She couldn't! Why—I just left her. You're lyin'— you're lyin'—just to kid me. Y' ain't? The same window? Oh, my God!

POST SCRIPT

SCENE: *The living room of Mrs. Matilda Clarkson.*

(*The room is indicated by a bridge table and chairs.* MRS. ADA ABBOTT *enters. She wears a fur neck piece, gloves, and a hat. She carries a hand bag, and talks busily.*)

Mattie, my dear—I'm so sorry, so dreadfully sorry—but I can't help it. The traffic . . . you know what traffic is! And the clock at home keeps gaining . . . and then when I get to counting on it, I find Jim has set it back.

(*She is taking off her gloves, fur, and hat and is putting them on the table. Suddenly she sees someone.*)

Oh, Harriet, dear . . . you're looking so well. Yes, indeed! And Mrs. Tillbury! I'm so glad you could give us to-day—and I do hope you'll be able to find out what's wrong with my bridge. I need help, don't I, Mattie? But, then, who doesn't?

Thank you, my dear, I will. (*She sits down at the table.*) Now . . . the sooner we get started the better, because I have to leave early, and since we're paying Mrs. Tillbury for the lesson, we ought to use

every minute of her. I can't help that, Mrs. Tillbury,
it's my Scotch blood.

But just while Mattie's getting out the cards I
want to read you something. (*She fumbles around in
her bag and brings out an envelope.*) One of Dick's
letters!

Dick is my son, Mrs. Tillbury. Of course, you don't
know him, but I can't help thinking you'll be interested. He writes so intelligently. He's the same age
as Mattie's Jack . . . so I knew she'd love to
hear. . . .

What's that, Mattie? Oh, it's quite short. It won't
take a minute. And it's so amusing . . . especially
the end!

You know how college boys are, Mrs. Tillbury.
Particularly Freshmen. (*From her bag she takes out
a pair of horn-rimmed spectacles.*) Of course, he's
been terribly homesick, but he manages to hide it in
his letters. Just the same, we know it's there.

(*She puts on the glasses, and reads.*)

"*Dear Muggie—*"

That's his pet name for me. Sometimes he calls me
Scotty, and sometimes Butts, but when he's feeling
particularly affectionate—or when he wants something—he calls me Muggie. You see, he's never been
like a son. Not in the least! More like a younger
brother.

Oh, Mattie, have you got the cards ready? Well,
just go ahead and deal. This won't take a minute.

"Dear Muggie: I haven't written for two weeks be-cause I have been studying day and night."

It's been much more than two weeks, really. It's been over a month. I was so worried I telephoned the college—eleven dollars' worth of long distance.

But of course, if he's studying day and night . . . It's simply terrible the way they work the boys now-a-days. Examinations all the time, and cramming way into the night—and then giving them bad marks any-way. Indeed they do, Harriet! Dick says almost no-body gets above a C. I don't know why. The profes-sors just don't give A's and B's any more. (*She reads again.*)

"And then I have not been feeling very well. Had a sort of a cold."

The poor boy never was very strong. I know he played on the football team at high school, Mattie, but that was sheer grit!

I'm surprised we managed to raise him at all, Mrs. Tillbury. The way he had measles! You remember Dick's measles, Harriet. Spots from head to foot! Mumps, too.

Yes, I know, Mattie, but your Jack didn't begin to have such a case. Well, I happen to be sure, because Dr. Eisen took care of both of them. He said he had never seen any mumps that *compared* with Dick's mumps. Never in his entire medical career!

Harriet, you really ought to give up coffee, or do something for your nerves. They're definitely jumpy!

Oh, have you got them all dealt? Well . . . well
—we'll have to start, won't we? I'll just skip through
the rest.

*"The weather has been very bad, too. It has rained
so much it was hard to mail letters."*

They have dreadful weather back there. Dreadful.
Often it rains so much he can't get to his classes.

"And then my typewriter broke down."

His father gave him a portable for Christmas. Of
course that may seem extravagant to you, Mrs. Tillbury, but we always had an idea Dick might be an
author some day. Yes. His Uncle John is an advertis-
ing man, so writing runs in the family, and you never
can tell when a thing like that might break out. So
we thought he'd better have a typewriter handy just
in case—

Yes, Harriet . . . I know. (*She picks up her
cards.*) I'll just glance through my hand. Well, this
certainly doesn't look like much! I do have the worst
luck, Mrs. Tillbury. I hope you can teach me how to
change it!

Now, while you're all deciding what to bid, I'll
give you the rest. I simply can't let you miss the end.
That's what's so screamingly funny—the post script.

*"Now I've got to stop this and go to the library.
It's getting along toward spring exams so I don't sup-
pose I'll be able to write so often the next few weeks.
Love to you both. Dick."*

And then down here—see? He's printed it in small capitals!

"P.S. NEED FIFTY DOLLARS."

There, isn't that just too delicious? Putting it in sort of casually like that? As if it didn't mean a thing? And he really can't, you know. I mean, he really can't need it. Because he had his allowance the first of the month, and then his father sent him an extra twenty, and I sent him ten—neither of us knew the other'd sent it. And we don't intend to send him another cent. Not another cent! Unless, of course, we decide he really needs it for something important.

Oh, my dears, are you waiting for *me?* I'm so sorry. Now . . . now . . . let me see. Who bid how much and what ought I to do about it? Oh, Mrs. Tillbury . . . I do hope you'll be able to find out what's wrong with my bridge!

IMPROBABLE INTERVIEW

SCENE: *A publisher's office.*

(MR. WILLIAMS, *the publisher, speaks to his most popular novelist.*)

> Listen, lady, if you must
> Pack your tale so full of lust,
> Full of sex, and girls betrayed,
> So that ninety in the shade
> Is its lowest temperature,
> Could you not within your pages
> Give us just one girl that's poor?
> One girl who her thirst assuages
> Not with champagne but with pure
> Sparkling water, and who stages
> Parties lacking in allure?
> Briefly, in your coming tome
> Couldn't just *one* girl walk home?